the ➡ RATING GAME

the RATING GAME

The Foolproof Formula for Finding Your Perfect Soul Mate

Reba Toney

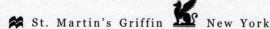 St. Martin's Griffin New York

www.stmartins.com

Book design by Jonathan Bennett

Library of Congress Cataloging-in-Publication Data

Toney, Reba.
    The rating game: the foolproof formula for finding your perfect soul mate/Reba Toney.—1st ed.
        p. cm.
    ISBN-13: 978-0-312-38398-5
    ISBN-10: 0-312-38398-3
1. Dating (Social customs).   2. Man-woman relationships.   I. Title.

HQ801 .T576 2009
646.7'7—dc22

2009006903

First Edition: June 2009

10   9   8   7   6   5   4   3   2   1

To Daisey,
without whom my singleness
would not have been
the same

Contents

Acknowledgments

THANK YOU TO my daughter, Daisey, for graciously allowing me time to write. Thanks to Wendy Keller for believing in me, Pam Liflander for being everything that I am not, Patrick Hennessy for encouragement, and Chuck Tyler for always supporting my efforts. Unending thanks to Dena, Tony, my mom, (step)dad, amazing friends, family, and ex-boyfriends for your love, prayers, and great dating stories. Thanks to God for never giving me more than I can bear.

Introduction

BACK IN 2004, my closet was already jam-packed. The last thing I needed was to make room for *another* unworn dress. Frustrated, I shoved all my clothes to one side so I could tuck the huge garment bag into the back where I wouldn't see it every day. I had just canceled another wedding. It was my fourth engagement and once again I just couldn't go through with it. It just wasn't the right guy again. That morning I received a copy of the DVD *Runaway Bride* from my mother. Her eccentric sense of humor has a way of snapping me back to reality. I sat at the foot of my bed wondering what I would do with another pair of beaded pumps.

I turned my personal inventory list from my closet to my love life. Both have some good pieces, but there is a whole lot of clutter. I'm good-looking but not perfect. I have an eclectic group of friends. I have a great job hosting a daily radio show in Los Angeles where I get to emcee concerts, travel with world relief organizations, raise money for local charities, and even work in television. I do fun things even though I've always been on a very tight budget.

The radio business is all flash, no cash. All of my work is fun, though it doesn't leave me a lot of personal time.

I also have a great daughter through a marriage that didn't work out. He was canceled wedding number one, and then we went through with it in wedding number two, and eventually split. Just like in my closet, in my life there's a lot to sort through, including my past relationships. When it comes to men, if you would put me in a room filled with a hundred guys, ninety-nine would be perfect for me, but I'd find the one that wasn't.

So back in my room I decided to pick myself up off my bed and begin a quest to find out how my qualities, including my faults, my strengths, my weaknesses, my likes and dislikes, all fit together. Then one day, it hit me like a brick. Rather than seeing myself as a whole person, I was focusing on my worst attributes. I realized that the men I dated didn't mind the parts of myself I disliked the most. I also noticed that I dated men who identified with my worst qualities, and a lot of the time, this feature turned out to be their best attribute. Even though these relationships always felt comfortable, they were never really exciting or inspiring. Ultimately, I would just get bored, and end up dumping these well-intentioned men. This left me with nothing less than the four wedding dresses now hanging in my closet, and a lot of perfectly-dyed-to-match white shoes.

If you lined up all the guys I've dated, it would seem like a completely random sample. There were tall ones and short ones, skinny and big, with long or short hair or bald, and of every color in the rainbow. The thing they all had in common was that in the end, I had to let them go, because I realized that none of them was good enough for me. I had created a dating pattern of "dating down." Because I was so overly concerned with my worst attributes, I wasn't ever showcasing the parts about me that I really liked. So I never attracted guys who would be interested in the best I had to offer.

On a few occasions, when the planets were all in alignment and my life was going great, I found myself in a situation where I was "dating up." Those relationships were fun at first because I felt good about myself when I dated guys who were really handsome or really buff. Now I realized that these guys were identifying only with my finest qualities. Yet it didn't take too much time for me to see that these boys couldn't tolerate the negative or mediocre things about me. In the end, those relationships made me feel bad about myself, and ended very quickly.

I needed to find a way for me to date men who were "on my level." And that's when *The Rating Game* was born. When I lined up my qualities—both good and bad—I found they fell into four categories. Using a simple scale of 1 to 10, I came up with my rating number. Then I went back over all of my past relationships and rated the men in my life. The numbers confirmed my suspicions. When I "dated down" and my numbers were higher than those of the guy I was dating, I always ended up doing the dumping. When I "dated up" and my numbers were lower, I usually got dumped. Finally, I could see right there on a single piece of paper why none of my past relationships ever worked out in the long run.

The next challenge was to find the men who matched my numbers. And that wasn't too hard at all: there are datable men everywhere! Over time, I found plenty of guys out there who were perfectly rated for me. The change has been remarkable and I have not ended up engaged to the wrong guy in years.

The Rating Game will help you assess yourself from head to toe, including your heart and soul. It will also show you how to see the men around you in the same light, so you can determine your dating range, leaving frustration and, hopefully, heartache behind. This book will introduce you to the four categories in the rating system. You'll learn how to rate yourself, and even how to make some quick corrections to get your numbers higher. You'll figure out how to set your own Personal Filter, so you'll be able to judge who is best for every facet of you! Next, you'll learn how to rate guys in an instant, and see if they are a potential match for you or if you need to weed them out of your life like that five-year-old shirt in the back of your closet. You'll begin to see each date for more than just his best or worst qualities. I'll even show you how this simple method can be used in any dating situation, from meeting guys randomly to getting fixed up by friends, or even for online dating.

LET'S START THE RATING GAME NOW

So where are you? Have you kicked so many guys to the curb that you wear steel-toed Pradas on Friday nights? Or are you making deals with God to offer your firstborn child to an ashram in India if only He would send you someone *decent* to date? Do you stare at your cell phone all night as if it is going to ring any moment, and even shake it just in case a text message got stuck? Are you thinking of filing a class action lawsuit against Verizon because they sold you a phone that won't let calls from men through? Or, are you so disillusioned that you've stopped dating altogether, bought a cat, and convinced yourselves that Mr. Puff-Puff is the only tom you'll ever need?

Sometimes finding the right guy feels as likely as the Hubble telescope finding a McDonald's in the Andromeda galaxy. If we're lucky, we pay attention to that "this isn't going to work out" feeling on the first or second date. I know I've been guilty of ignoring the signs, and hanging on to bad relationships for months, even years, hoping or trying to get him to change, or trying to live up to his expectations. Eventually I would find myself back at square one. But not anymore! Now, if the numbers don't work for me, I know that the relationship isn't going to survive. I'm able to walk away without investing so much of myself, which leaves me feeling empowered, and ready to find another guy who may be better suited for me.

It is my hope that you will use this book as your GPS for your dating journey. No one can guarantee "happily ever after," but *The Rating Game* will surely improve your odds! Best of all, you might find out something new about yourself: something that you really like. So have fun, and start rating!

—REBA TONEY

the ➤ RATING GAME

I.

Dating Up and Dating Down

Are You Dating Up or Down?

Which situation best describes your last relationship?

1. I broke up with him
2. I got dumped
3. I haven't been in a relationship for two years or longer

What emotion best describes how you felt during your last relationship?

1. Disappointed
2. Inadequate
3. Lonely

Did you feel like the person in your relationship had . . .

1. Potential
2. Everything
3. Nothing at all

Which best describes the way you met?

1. He approached me first
2. I approached him first
3. We were just friends before ending up together

Which describes how you felt about yourself when you met him?

1. Feeling great about life
2. In a weird place
3. Have no idea what I was thinking

What adjective best describes your first date?

1. Disappointing
2. Dreamy
3. Impersonal

Did you feel like the relationship was . . .

1. Doomed
2. Destined
3. What relationship?

What did you wear on your average night out with him?

1. Whatever I wore to work that day
2. Another brand-new outfit
3. Old jeans and a T-shirt

How important was sex and intimacy in this relationship?

1. I wasn't too interested in having a physical relationship
2. I was ready to have sex all the time to make him happy
3. What's sex?

What type of fruit would best describe your last boyfriend?

1. Mealy apples on sale
2. Perfect peaches at $4.99 a pound
3. Sorry: out of stock

If you answered mainly 1s you are the dumper, and need to stop dating down.

If you answered mainly 2s you are the dumped, and need to stop dating up.

If you answered mainly 3s you are in dating denial, or are not dating enough.

Why is dating so darn difficult? Maybe it's our surreal expectations. Rarely is a personal association as closely scrutinized. Every call, every word, every kiss, and every dinner is put under a microscope and analyzed in an attempt to find a hidden meaning. And what do we end up discovering, Sherlock? Most of the time, what you see is what you get.

Other social activities have a learning curve. Usually an activity requires a bit of practice before you get really good at it, but every time you try, you build on your past experience. Take volleyball, for instance: when you started back in eighth grade, you played in a few games, you figured out how the team scores, and after you realized how boring it was, you got smart and brought a note into gym class saying you were having your period. Or, after a couple of games you got the hang of it, and figured out how to duck out of the way when a ball was coming toward your head.

But dating is different. First, every person is different, so every relationship will be different (don't you hate that?). That means there isn't really a lot of room for practice, because you never get the same ball thrown at you. And, although we may think we learn a lot from relationships that don't work out, what we learn isn't always applicable. For instance, if you found out that your last date was previously an ax murderer, what are the chances that you'll meet another guy like that?

The real tragedy here is that on those rare occasions when we could actually learn from our mistakes, we miss the message entirely. Instead, most of us operate the way I used to, and continue to repeat our dating mistakes. We choose the same type of person again and again, and then we are surprised when yet another relationship turns out to have the same bad ending. No sooner do we get good at dating than we turn around to witness the sea of failed relationships in our wake. Then you ask, "Why am I doomed to attend events with my cousin?"

RELATIONSHIPS THAT WILL NEVER WORK OUT

I've found that there are three types of bad relationships. The first is when you are *dating up*. Dating up occurs when you are constantly dating people who are "above" you in some area of life, whether it's their extreme good looks, a fabulous body, a dynamic personality, or a life situation (i.e., great career, lots of money). You know that you are dating up if you are always getting dumped: eventually, the person you're dating realizes that he is "too good" for you. This doesn't mean that you shouldn't have aspirations, but it does mean that you need to be a little more realistic about what you are bringing to the dating table.

On the other hand, if you are always dumping the men you date, then you are *dating down:* you're choosing guys who really are not good enough for you. You're dating down if you are constantly bored in your relationships. Or, you may be subconsciously looking for someone to mother, or smother, until you realize that each guy is a project you aren't willing to complete.

And if you are not dating at all, it is likely that you have a misconception about how fabulous, or unfabulous, you really are. Or, if you do realize what you've got, you might not want to date people who are in the same boat. I call either of these scenarios *dating denial*. And I find that with rare exceptions (as in Cinderella and/or Prince Charming), dating denial will also lead to dead ends or problematic relationships.

Dating up, dating down, or dating denial are all clear signs of being stuck in a rut. You might have a lot to offer, but you have gotten comfortable choosing—or being chosen by—the wrong person. I'm going to show you how you can stop this cycle, get out of your dating rut, and start dating guys who are just right for you.

THE MISSING SOCK DILEMMA

In America, 40 percent of adults are single. That is a lot of lonely socks to sort through. So if you are having trouble finding a match, then you may be what I consider a "frustrated dater." Sometimes, dating is like trying to put together a piece of furniture from IKEA. You open the box, lay out all the parts, and look at the pictogram instructions—but no matter how hard you try, the new entertainment stand just isn't coming together. You know that "other people" bought the same furniture, and in fact, they are very happy with it. Were they smarter? Not likely. Chances are they were simply better at putting stuff together. So now think of reading this book as taking another shot at putting your life together. By carefully reading these dating instructions, you'll be able to find plenty of matches in the pile of lonely socks.

It is equally frustrating when you have not been approached by someone of the opposite sex in a long, long time. You might feel like you live in a town where there is not a decent single guy left. But I can assure you that there is still hope, even if you are an extremely frustrated dater. There are plenty of good men out there. In the meantime, here's what you need to do when you are frustrated with dating (or frustrated with not dating):

- Find one married person you can call who will tell you their problems. This will give you a new perspective on being single.

- Go out to dinner with your favorite couple. You will get the "relationship feeling" through osmosis.

- Start opening your mail at a nearby coffee shop. You will feel less lonely doing routine tasks around others. While you're at it, start doing your laundry at the local Laundromat for another social setting.

- Don't go home after work. Go anywhere else but home for at least four hours. It will break up your week.

WHY AREN'T YOU DATING?
Have you used any of the following "legitimate reasons" for why you're not dating?

- I haven't been asked out
- I don't know anyone
- There is not anyone I'm interested in
- I don't like myself right now

- I don't have any money to go out
- No one would like me
- I'm raising kids
- Asking someone out gives me hives
- I work too much
- I wouldn't know where to start
- People scare me
- I need to lose weight first
- I'm too old
- I'm not pretty enough
- Who would want me?
- There is no one good-looking at my age
- I don't know any single people
- I have too much baggage
- I'm not in a good place right now
- I'm in school right now
- I live with my parents
- I'm consumed with addictions
- I don't leave my house
- I will soon
- My best days are behind me

IF YOU *ARE* DATING

Let's get to the lowdown on why you are dating. What are your goals in a relationship? You may be saying, "Reba, who cares what my goals are? I just want someone to take me to the movies." But I'll tell you who should care: you. The men out there can sense what you are really looking for, and will respond to your wishes.

They are like puppies: eager to please. The one who is looking for the same type of relationship will be the one who is attracted to you. But if you don't know what you are looking for, or why you are looking, you can cast your line all day and never get a nibble.

There are more reasons for dating than there are stars in the sky. When you were in your teens, you may have started dating by identifying the qualities that you like in other people (or to experiment with your budding sexuality). As you get older, after a divorce, or even during a busy time in your life, you may date simply for companionship. Are you looking for someone to spend the rest of your life with, or do you just want to sample what's out there? See if you can identify with any of the following descriptions. You might find that at different times in your life, you might have been many of these daters. But we're living in the present: look for where you want to be right now. Then I can show you how to get there.

THE MONOGAMIST

Looking for long-term love and acceptance; wanting to find someone to explore deep feelings and emotions in a trusting environment. Welcome to Loyal Heart Village. If you find love here, you can look forward to a lifetime of memories, some good and some bad, but a committed partner to see you through it all.

THE BUSINESS PARTNER

Looking for someone to share domestic duties, expenses, and occasional sex. I now pronounce you Mr. and Mrs. Joint Venture. Combining domestic and career skills can make for a very productive relationship.

THE FAMILY PLANNER

Looking to fill the role of husband or parent. Required husband duties include car maintenance, lawn care, parenting, and additional income. In exchange, you need to be willing to provide hot meals, bedroom fun, and family vacations. Knowing exactly what you want in life is very prudent and can yield a relationship that ticks like clockwork.

THE ONE-NIGHTER

Looking for a pleasant evening and good company, taking one day at a time. Knowing that you have just one night with someone who could be so much more can be wonderfully adventurous and invigorating. The trick is to avoid the dreaded "walk of shame" by not getting too physical with someone you'll never date again.

THE AUTO PILOT

Looking for something, but not sure exactly what it is—there really is no motive or conscious thought when dating, just hoping to hook someone or get hooked. If this is your M.O., see if you are the apple that didn't fall far from the tree. Maybe dear

REBA'S GOLDEN RULE:
It's Better to Date Well Than to Date Often

There is a difference between dating and devouring. For me, the ground rule of dating is that you should meet people with the intention of giving and receiving. It's not enough to be constantly taking something from someone, which is why I do not consider hook-ups as dating. Hook-ups are all about what you can get, not what you can give.

The length of time you date someone is not important. Neither is the number of dates you have each week, or each month. The questions you need to answer for each relationship you enter are: Are you giving or taking? Is it all about a free dinner, or are you learning something new about yourself? Are you giving positive attention? Are you having fun?

If you approach each dating opportunity as a new chance to give, then you will feel good about dating, and you'll start having fun. You'll enjoy sharing the best parts of you. Plus, when we give we grow.

ol' mom or dad was your role model for relationships. If you are on this path, at least you know exactly where it leads.

THE RECREATIONAL PARTNER

Looking for someone to have dinner or see a movie with, or take to a family wedding. Having a reliable date for events is highly underrated. If you find a good backup guy (let's call him Date #2), keep him on speed dial.

STOP LEAVING YOUR LOVE LIFE TO CHANCE

Are you in dating denial because you are hoping that you'll just bump into the perfect guy? Or are you trying to maximize your face time, getting out into the world and meeting as many people as you can? You may believe that you'll "run into" the man of your dreams, but don't be surprised if you are just doing a lot of running.

Dating is not governed by the laws of Las Vegas, though I do love Las Vegas. So don't peg your hopes on the gambler's fallacy. This unwritten rule is based on the fact that gamblers often believe that random events happen for a reason, such as "a run of (good or bad) luck," or a mistaken understanding of "the law of averages." It simply isn't true that a random event, like meeting the perfect guy by chance, can be affected by or predicted from other, independent events. It is not more likely to occur because it happened once before; nor is it more likely to occur because it has *not* happened recently.

The reality is that there is really no such thing as chance when it comes to dating. People who date well do more than create their own good luck: they make a conscious effort in choosing the right men to pursue, and choosing the best places to be to meet them. And even though it may *seem* like your dating life is like a spin of the roulette wheel, the truth is that we are all creatures of habit. Otherwise what are the odds that you would "just happen" to be meeting the same type of guy over and over again?

BUT HE SEEMED NICE WHEN I MET HIM

We all develop communication strategies early in life, and we stick with them. If we were given the same polite greeting from fifteen different people, we would most likely respond the same way each time. It's the difference between saying "What's up?" while others say, "Hey" or "How's it going?" We also have set patterns that direct our behaviors, especially in the ways we approach others, or allow ourselves to be approached. Our set behaviors will be attractive to a few types of people, just as their behaviors may or may not be attractive to you. But just because someone responds to your behaviors positively doesn't mean that you should pursue that person. While it is fun and very flattering to have a person show interest, it is not enough to roll the dice and hope we will not get hurt.

Many who are dating by chance are willing to place their bets as if they have nothing to lose. That's not true, either. While dating is not usually much of a monetary risk, you are putting yourself, and your heart, on the table. A broken heart will eventually heal, but the scars can last. Sometimes there is so much scar tissue that it keeps real affection from reaching us again.

ARE YOU IN DATING DENIAL?

On the other hand, we have to be reasonable about our dating choices. If you aren't dating because "there isn't anyone around worth dating," you may end up spending your whole life alone. Dating denial clouds our minds, and we soon begin to think that our mildest accomplishments or nominal good looks have us in line for a relationship with our favorite celebrity. If you are waiting for near perfection to knock on the door, think again: Matthew McConaughey is not dropping by. Instead, open yourself to the possibility that you might want to date the men who want to date you. Not that you should date anyone who wants to date you, but you can at least find someone you want that also wants you. You may want McConaughey but he wants Brazilian models, so that's not going to work.

Dating denial is a terrible place to be because it limits us, and can even stop us from dating altogether. If you are in dating denial you will never notice the datable people around you because you are too busy thinking that you deserve so much more. If you are waiting for red carpet good looks, then here is the kink in your logic: celebrities are actors who *pretend* to be normal people. But in reality they are not normal people. They are the crème de la crème of good-looking hotties who are *pretending* to have normal flaws and shortcomings in their movies and TV shows. Sure they are human, but Jen Aniston never had to work at Central Perk and she's not really interested in Monica's brother.

Dating denial basically means that you are not being honest with yourself regarding the people you are suited to date. For example, do you still see yourself with the face and body you had ten years ago? Do you still think you can snag the same type of man you were interested in ten years ago? Get ready for this news flash: we have changed since high school. The type of guy that we are suited for has also changed. We should not expect to attract a current quarterback playing on any professional, college, or high school team.

We will only sink deeper into dating denial if we don't allow ourselves to change. It is like when people get stuck in a clothing style from when they were at the height of trendiness. Have you ever seen an older woman who still sports a beehive hairdo because that's what she wore back in the day when she was really popular? I want to run down the street after her and gently tell her that it's time to grow up. So I'll tell you instead: if you can allow yourself the opportunity to change, you may just find that you'll be popular again.

It is not just looks that keep us in denial. Sometimes we are impressed with our IQ or our bank account. Each of these aspects of ourselves needs to be put in perspective with our other attributes, so that we don't price ourselves out of our dating market. Pricing yourself out of your dating range means that you think so highly of yourself that no one could ever be good enough, which is a really effective way to end up alone, or once again dating up or down. It's like the attitude of the overbearing mother, Marie, of the hit TV show *Everybody Loves Raymond*. Marie tries to find things that she does not like about Raymond's wife, Debra, not because she doesn't like Debra but because she doesn't think anyone is good enough for her son. If you price yourself out of the dating market then you will always find things that you don't like about the guys around you simply because you think no one is good enough for you.

So, we need to get real about who we are, right now (especially if you have a shelf full of moisturizers and a drawer full of push-up bras). Having a good job is great but it does not define us. Having blond hair is fantastic but it is not representative of your whole self. If you ask really good-looking people how much looks matter in their life they will usually say, "Not much." That's because they know that they are more than just a pretty face. A lot of attractive people tell me that their looks sometimes become a stumbling block for people to get to know the real them. It also holds true for people with a lot of money: if you ask them they will tell you at the end of the day money can't buy happiness. In our hearts we all know that we are so much more than any one attribute we have. The fact is we are a combination of all of our attributes. The combination is what makes us all unique and different.

I know that it can be scary to look at ourselves in the "big picture." Instead, we focus on one great attribute instead of facing the rest of our less favorable qualities. This can be an optimist's idea of being positive—in an attempt to not beat yourself up, you neglect whole parts of yourself in fear of having a real weakness. Seeing the good or even great qualities we have can mean that we have a lot to live up to, which is why some women lowball their standards. They may feel that they really have to be perfect in every area of life in order to have anything to offer someone else.

For others it is the exact opposite. Some women so closely scrutinize their negative qualities it's as if seeing the good in themselves would be a mortal sin. These "glass half empty" women are constantly obsessing about their faults, justifying that if only they were different their lives would be more perfect. They are making the same mistake that I made. Instead of facing who I really was, I focused on what I perceived were my imperfections. But by doing so I was ignoring who I really was, and what I had to offer. The truth is that we all have a beautiful array of strengths and weakness. We each offer more in some areas and less in others, and that's okay. Having a variety of attributes is a part of being human. Maybe we will all be perfect in heaven, but until then embrace the fact that we are all beautifully flawed.

Dating denial is one of the most important reasons why we must learn how to properly assess ourselves. Having the wrong idea about who you are is the first thing standing in your way of having a great relationship. When the view you have of yourself is skewed, then your perception of the type of people who will make you happy becomes tainted too. We must see ourselves for who we are so we can find an appropriate match, because if your favorite nighttime sitcom heartthrob doesn't come calling, you have to be able to find happiness some other way.

The following appeared on Craigslist, and is a great example of someone in deep dating denial:

"What Am I Doing Wrong?" by Miss Twenty-five
Okay, I'm tired of beating around the bush. I'm a beautiful (spectacularly beautiful) twenty-five-year-old girl. I'm articulate and classy. I'm not from New York. I'm looking to get married to a guy who makes at least half a million a year. I know how that sounds, but keep in mind that a million a year

is middle class in New York City, so I don't think I'm over-reaching at all.

Are there any guys who make $500,000 or more on this board? Any wives? Could you send me some tips? I dated a businessman who makes an average of around $200,000 to $250,000. But that's where I seem to hit a roadblock. Making $250,000 won't get me to Central Park West. I know a woman in my yoga class who was married to an investment banker and lives in Tribeca, and she's not as pretty as I am, nor is she a great genius. So what is she do-ing right? How do I get to her level?

Here are my questions specifically:

- Where do you single rich men hang out? Give me specifics—bars, restaurants, gyms.

- What are you looking for in a mate? Be honest, guys, you won't hurt my feelings.

- Is there an age range I should be targeting? (I'm twenty-five.)

- Why are some of the women living lavish lifestyles on the Upper East Side so plain? I've seen really Plain Jane boring types who have nothing to offer married to incredibly wealthy guys. I've seen drop-dead gorgeous girls in singles bars in the East Village. What's the story there?

- Jobs I should look out for? Everyone knows—lawyer, investment banker, doctor. How much do those guys really make? And where do they hang out? Where do the hedge fund guys hang out?

- How you decide marriage versus just a girlfriend? I am looking for *marriage only*.

The Answer From Mr. Superficial

Dear Miss Twenty-five:

I read your posting with great interest and have thought meaningfully about your dilemma. I offer the following analysis of your predicament. Firstly, I'm not wasting your time, I qualify as a guy who fits your bill; that is I make more than $500,000 per year. That said, here's how I see it.

Your offer, from the prospective [*sic*] of a guy like me, is plain and simple a crappy business deal. Here's why. Cutting through all the bullshit, what you suggest is a simple trade: you bring your looks to the party and I bring my money. Fine, simple. But here's the rub, your looks will fade and my money will likely continue into perpetuity . . . in fact, it is very likely that my income increases but it is an absolute certainty that you won't be getting any more beautiful!

So, in economic terms you are a depreciating asset and I am an earning asset. Not only are you a depreciating asset, your depreciation accelerates! Let me explain: you're twenty-five now and will likely stay pretty hot for the next five years, but less so each year. Then the fade begins in earnest. By thirty-five, stick a fork in you! So in Wall Street terms, we would call you a trading position, not a buy and hold . . . hence the rub . . . marriage. It doesn't make good business sense to "buy you" (which is what you're asking) so I'd rather lease. In case you think I'm being cruel, I would say the following: if my money were to go away, so would you, so when your beauty fades I need an out. It's as simple as that. So a deal that makes sense is dating, not marriage.

Separately, I was taught early in my career about efficient markets. So, I wonder why a girl as "articulate, classy, and spectacularly beautiful" as you has been unable to find your sugar daddy. I find it hard to believe that if you are as gorgeous as you say you are that the $500K hasn't found you, if not only for a tryout.

By the way, you could always find a way to make your own money and then we wouldn't need to have this difficult conversation.

With all that said, I must say you're going about it the right way. I hope this is helpful, and if you want to enter into some sort of lease, let me know.

The problem with this correspondence is that Mr. Superficial is dead wrong. While he thought he had everything figured out, he was in as much dating denial as Miss Twenty-five. Both were evaluating their dating potential by counting on their best traits. Miss Twenty-five is assessing herself on her looks. And while the Plain Janes she speaks so negatively about may not be as beautiful as she is, they probably have great personalities or life situations. Miss Twenty-five is overly impressed with her strengths and neglecting her weaknesses.

On the flip side, Mr. Superficial is taking the bait and also judging her solely on her looks, which he believes will fade. So he's wrong on many counts. First, we all know that beautiful young women can get more beautiful as they age, with or without the help of a genius plastic surgeon. Second, women are more than just their beauty. Every person has love, wisdom, memories, joy, truth, heartache, and soul to give. For a man to say a woman only brings her looks to the table makes him a shallow jerk. And frankly, for Miss Twenty-five to be banking on her looks alone leaves her in dating denial, or, as she says herself, not dating at all.

My heart breaks for all the girls who read the response to this article and felt their self-worth plummet. I also feel mortified that any woman would post an ad asking for a new life situation! It's as if a man comes with the life situation, instead of the life situation coming with a man.

Jamie

Jamie is a strikingly beautiful actress with an amazing personality. People will literally chase her down to tell her how beautiful she is. She told me the story of her first love when she moved to New York City. Martin was everything to her. He was excessively attractive and successful. The pair looked to be the perfect match, but he annoyed her with his constant references to his Ivy League education and blue blood. Martin wanted Jamie to be an intellectual and social equal, and eventually the two went their separate ways.

After the breakup, Jamie spiraled into a depression. Her modeling and acting career had forced her to skip college when she was younger, and she began worrying that all the men she would meet would think that she was stupid. Worse, Jamie was haunted by the fact that she didn't come from an affluent family. Her beauty became a worthless asset in her mind.

I reminded Jamie that her beauty was not worthless, but she had mistakenly banked on her looks for too long. She had spent so much time judging herself solely by her reflection in the mirror that she was shocked when men wanted something else. She thought she was a great catch because of her face and body and hoped that would be enough to snag Mr. Wonderful. Yet even though Martin was initially attracted to her because of her looks, in the end he was interested in a package that Jamie couldn't offer. I told Jamie that her answer to this problem is to learn how to understand her whole self, and everything she had to give to a relationship. I taught her the secrets of the Rating Game, and today, Jamie is no longer insecure about her past. Instead, she knows what she has to offer, and meets plenty of men who are interested—and interesting.

IT ALL CHANGES WITH THE RATING GAME

My method is going to change your whole outlook on dating, and help you get a better perspective on yourself and the rest of the dating world. It will immediately stop you from dating up or dating down. Best of all, you'll break out of your dating denial, because you'll know how to instantly and accurately assess potential dates so that you can see them in their entirety. That way you won't get hooked on a guy who's funny but doesn't have a job, or has money and is mean. You'll learn to see men for who they are as a whole.

The system is simple, and you start with yourself. You are the filter by which you measure others, so this method is really about how you see the world. I am going to teach you how to assess all of your attributes, as well as the attributes of others, and limit the math to four easy categories. Once you know where you rate you will feel more comfortable dating, because you will learn to match up with people in your range. So while different people will have different standards, and different ratings, you'll learn how to apply your standards to everyone in your dating world. Ultimately, you'll find that dating this way is a lot more fun.

Are You Dating Down, Up, or in Dating Denial?

See if any of the following actually are swimming around your head when you are on a date. They are indicative of your dating patterns.

If these sound familiar, you have Dating Down Deep Secret Thoughts:

- I wish you would talk more when we're out with my friends
- You would look better in a different style
- Your car embarrasses me
- Anything with the P word, "potential": I thought you had more potential
- The furniture in your apartment makes me want to throw up

If you are thinking of saying what follows, you have Dating Up Deep Secret Thoughts:

- Quit nagging me
- If I could do it better I would
- I don't understand

- This is all I have to wear
- Overuse of the S word, "sorry": as in "I'm sorry you don't like my dress"

If these come to mind, you have Dating Denial Deep Secret Thoughts:

- The hair on my legs is getting so long
- My passenger seat is full of junk
- I spend most of my time at work
- My freezer is full of Lean Cuisine
- Evening wear, what's that?

THE RATING GAME ENDS DESPERATION DATING

None of us likes to hear the *D* word but leaving dating to chance is a desperate move. Desperate times do not have to mean desperate measures. *We all get lonely sometimes, but don't throw away your good judgment, ambition, or even personal wisdom for companionship.*

I know that it can be hard to take a step back when we are so intent on moving forward. Unfortunately until now there has been no way to evaluate our dating decisions. We have been blindly feeling our way around the dating world without Braille. We have been making decisions on the biggest relationships in our life based on a whim. *We do more research about a two-hour movie than about giving someone our phone numbers or access to our hearts.* Fortunately, my method will keep you from making a desperate move. Instantly you'll be able to see if any potential date is worth your time.

Mona

Mona was desperate for a lot of things, but this time she needed a plumber. Everything seemed normal when the leggy marketing director for a Fortune 500 company parked her 6 Series in her garage. As she made her way through the backyard she noticed that the gardener had ignored an overgrown fern that morning in his weekly tending. Mona then entered her condo and threw her fabulously large designer handbag on the dinette. That's when she noticed something really out of the ordinary.

Her bathroom was completely flooded, and water was dripping from the ceiling. There was brown, rusted water sitting two inches deep in her newly remodeled marble-everything bathroom. She immediately remembered that her neighbors in the unit above her were having plumbing work done. Even though it was late in the day, Mona managed to reach her neighbors, and the plumbers. They told her that it was after hours but they would send Alex to clean up and make sure her bathroom was working.

Mona wanted to run as far as she could from the nightmarish situation in her bathroom, but she knew that she had to wait to let Alex into the house. Mona grabbed her gardening shears and made a beeline for that overgrown fern in the backyard. She did not have much experience pruning but she had plenty of pent-up aggression, which she gladly bestowed upon that plant.

Meanwhile, Alex the plumber was at the gym when he got the after-hours call. He decided to head right over in his gym clothes. Mona heard the gate shut and turned to see a tall, muscular man in gym shorts and a clinging gray T-shirt standing in her backyard with a hose and a tool kit. Mona was very glad to see him. She let him into the house and ushered him toward the bathroom. She stood in the foyer and chatted with him, and pointed toward the bathroom disaster. Mona noticed his very symmetrical face before Alex let out nothing more than a grunt and lugged his equipment into the bathroom.

Mona continued to terrorize the fern in the backyard, but this time her pent-up aggression was a little bit different. She began thinking how cut Alex's body was. She was not expecting a cute guy with tan calves to be at her house. She was attracted to him, but could his biceps and sharp jawline compensate for his grunting?

Should Mona make the next move? Even though Alex was good-looking, built, and there, she knew that he really wasn't a match for Mona's sophisticated lifestyle. What's a desperate woman to do?

The answer is to rate him. In seconds Mona can decide if she's interested in him as a whole person or if she's just mesmerized by his bulging biceps. Maybe it will be a ripped plumber that wins Mona's heart, but she'll need to figure that out for herself. With the Rating Game you will learn that when you stop seeing one attribute as an avenue toward your happiness, or as potential on which to base a relationship, you will make better choices in your dating life.

THE RATING GAME WORKS FOR EVERYONE

Leaving reason behind for an encounter of the heart is not a sign of relational ambition; it is a sign of relational recklessness. Just do the math. No matter what your current situation is, this book will work for you. If you are divorced, a senior, a single parent, or have not been dating because of your career, the Rating Game will help you start dating the way you want to.

THE DIVORCED DATER

Divorce can sometimes feel like a black mark on your dating dance card, but there are certain factors and variables that can be taken into account for both the positives and the negatives. On the positive side, there is much wisdom gained from having been part of a committed relationship. On the negative side, it can be hard to muster up a second helping of a "this will last forever" attitude, after one marriage obviously did not. Sometimes the positives will cancel out the negatives, and other times they won't. But if you are strong enough to make it through a divorce, chances are that you are strong enough to get your life back together and ready to begin dating someone you will be truly happy with.

The Rating Game will make dating easier for you to get back out in the arena because postdivorce is the perfect time to take inventory of where you are at. Chances are that your rating will look a lot different than it did before you got married. There will be aspects of your life that have changed for the worse, and some that have changed for the better.

THE SENIOR DATER

At the intersection of increased life expectancy and greater quality of life is a place called retirement. You're feeling healthy, looking good, and slightly older, wiser, and having a lot of free time on your hands. This is the senior dater. More and more seniors have become part of the dating landscape. The great thing about being a dating senior is that "baggage" is out and "life experience" is in. For a senior who is dating it's all about having loved, lost, and lived. Being sixty-five-plus is like having a giant canvas splashed with paint. Diversity, family, and careers are brilliant colors to be relished. The only real folly is to have aged and not lived.

The Rating Game will show you how your perspective changes as you get older. That is why it is so important to rate others through your own filter. Your ideal of a perfect mate may have changed significantly over the years, and my system will help you assess what your needs are right now.

THE AMBITIOUS DATER

These little busy bees are always working. First there was school . . . undergrad, graduate, and possibly a lengthy internship. Then you went on to climbing that darn corporate ladder, always feeling that getting ahead came before falling in love. It was never the right time to settle down into a relationship.

I've heard it said that there are two types of men: those who want a princess to build their kingdom for, and those who want to build a kingdom and then find a queen. The latter is surely the lonelier path. The irony is that it is thought that men age better than women, even though they die a lot sooner. It seemingly puts the queen who has put love on hold until she acquires her kingdom at a disadvantage.

The Rating Game is imperative for Ms. Ambition. Your career successes may be impressive but your ability to focus so much time and attention on your career can actually reflect negatively on your personality and life situation in a dating relationship. Rating yourself will give you perspective on your emotional availability so you can see why it's important to put your work aside, just for a little while, and get out there and date.

THE SINGLE PARENT DATER

Single parents never really feel like they are single. They are always in a committed relationship, albeit to someone much younger. Single parents have so much to give, but the hard part for them is finding the time to talk to someone their own age. Not only do you have to deal with all your child's needs, you have to deal with finding a new guy as well. And as soon as your date notices the crayons in your purse, you've got to explain why you're not free on weekdays and need seventy-two hours' notice to secure your favorite babysitter.

Anyone will tell you that being a parent is life-changing. Developing a consciousness for someone else's needs and having to step outside of yourself are some of the biggest growth processes we experience. Parents learn from their children and see the world in a different type of glory. While a person can benefit from being a parent, there is no doubt that your dating needs will drastically change how you see life.

Rating yourself will help you document the ups and downs of single parenting. There is no other person in the world that needs a boost more than a person who is pouring their heart into the lives of children on a daily basis. You probably know your shortcomings and have probably already dwelled on your problems. My system will allow you to take some time to look over your best qualities and see how they add to your overall self. This will help you build your confidence to get out there and start dating again!

THIS IS GOING TO BE FUN

The Rating Game will change everything you thought about dating. Whether you are dating for short-term companionship or long-term commitment, you can use the system to get to the millions of men that are best suited for you. Not only will the Rating Game give you the tools to decipher what you really want, it will help you gain self-awareness about who you are and what you have to offer.

2.

Who Are You Looking For?

W E MAY BE all the same in God's eyes, and I'm sure your mom thinks there is no one better than you, but we're not trying to date God or your mom. The dating world is like the job market: there are always going to be applicants who are overqualified, underqualified, and just right. I'm not asking you to judge someone's worth to the planet or how much love they are entitled to, but to simply determine if they might be right for you.

But before I reveal the rules for rating, you first have to decide exactly who your ideal guy really is. To determine this, you'll use a well-honed sense of judgment that has been uniquely formulated by your Personal Filter. By practicing with these tools, you'll get a better understanding for the method behind your madness in terms of how you will rate men, as well as how you will rate yourself.

YOUR PERSONAL FILTER

Computers need both hardware and software in order to operate. The hardware gives the computer the ability to function; the software gives the computer the set of specific tasks. I've also found that there is hardware and software to dating. Think of your Personal Filter as the software, and the Rating Game as your hardware. Your Personal Filter allows you to perform a systems check on your ability to rate, making sure there are no bugs or kinks that will keep you from meeting the right guys, and making the best impression with them.

Your Personal Filter is an inherent system of standards or beliefs that you have about yourself and other people based on your past experiences, present situation, and future expectations. Your Personal Filter helps you navigate your world, as well as form impressions about others. In terms of the Rating Game, it helps you focus on and assess the characteristics in the four main areas. For example, in the face category, your Personal Filter is what helps you to determine if you are attracted to the clean-cut preppy or a long-haired rock star; an athletic build or a bookworm; a hip-hop prince or Nashville's country music look. Similarly, your Personal Filter will help you evaluate different body shapes, personalities, and life situations. For instance, some women would love to meet a career-driven corporate type, while others want to hang with the Rastafarians.

Lastly, don't assume that you will have the same Personal Filter as those around you, even your best girlfriends. To do so could land you in an unsatisfying relationship again. Only you know what you really want in a date, and who is right for you. If you explore these ideals honestly, I can guarantee that they won't look the same as anyone else's. And that's positive, because there are certainly many men out there who are just right for you.

There is a three-step process that will help you determine how you acquired your Personal Filter. Each step is used to help you evaluate each of the four categories in the Rating Game. Sounds confusing? It isn't. These steps will just show you where your thinking comes from, so your ratings don't seem so left field later in the process.

Byron

Byron is a perfect example of how different people's Personal Filters can affect their rating system. Byron had been working on his body as long as he could remember. The six foot body builder has legs like tree trunks. His square jaw and inviting smile are supported by a thick muscular neck. Byron views his huge buff body and symmetrically angled face as perfect. Byron is also very proud of his charitable giving. In fact, within minutes of meeting someone new, he'll tell them all about the families he supports and exactly how. Byron thinks very highly of himself, but when Lily first met him, she saw him quite differently. She saw his big body as bulky and his thick neck as overworked. She thought his angular face was good-looking but his clean-cut hair and shaved face were signs he was trying too hard. She liked his positive outlook, but found him to be too boastful.

Who was right? The answer is that they both were. Lily and Byron won't make a great couple, because they don't share the same values. Byron and Lily had completely different Personal Filters.

Patricia

Patricia used a lull in her social life to make some improvements to herself. This beautiful blonde was slightly more than fifty when she took advantage of her home equity line of credit and had a doctor freshen up some of the lines around her eyes and forehead. At the same time, her confidence soared as she parlayed her success as an administrative assistant into a lucrative sales position. Patricia's relationships with her kids and grandkids had never been better, and she found herself wanting a man in her life again.

Patricia had lived through several marriages herself, but she was sure she was now in a better place and ready to have a healthy, long-lasting relationship. She was not interested in anyone at her church, and she didn't really meet men anywhere else. So she took matters into her own hands and created a plan of action: she went online. She was surprised by the number of potential daters she had access to. She quickly connected with Frankie, a man about her age who lived thirty miles away. She decided to meet him for coffee. He was tall and friendly, so she decided to see him again.

The relationship progressed very quickly and Patricia soon found herself face-to-face with Frankie's flaws. And because she had such a good makeover, she asked him to fix little things about himself. She was hoping that they would be good together, but when he didn't want to change, Patricia found that she was constantly disappointed.

She told herself that this inequity didn't matter, because she hadn't been with a man in so long. She convinced herself that Frankie had the potential to be better and that they would be perfect together. But after a six-month relationship and near engagement, Patricia was having a hard time hanging on, and because she had invested so much of herself, she was also having a hard time letting go.

In this instance, Patricia realized that this relationship wasn't going to work out because Frankie wasn't the man she was looking for if he wouldn't make the changes she required. The fact that she wanted him to change shows that she was not in touch with her Personal Filter. The point of the Personal Filter is to set the ideal for what you value and then see how both you and your date stack up.

STEP ONE: LEARNING FROM YOUR PAST

Your Personal Filter was first created by what you have already absorbed in your past. Our earliest memories help us develop our likes and dislikes, as well as the intricate map needed to navigate relationships. The routines and surroundings of our youth typically become important aspects of our Personal Filter.

What were the surroundings of your past where you were the happiest? Were you living in a city, the suburbs, or something more rural? Did you have a large or small family? What was the mood of your family life: was it happy, fun, intense, or carefree? What were your role models like, especially your male role models? Were they athletes, musicians, workers, young or old people?

Now, think about whether you want to repeat any of these aspects of your past, or if you are looking for a relationship that will take you away from your past? Are you looking for someone "just like Dad" in every respect, or someone completely different? Do you want to live near your hometown, or are you ready to plunge into the great wide world? Are you looking for someone to bring into the family business, or are you attracted to someone who is self-made or ready to strike out on their own?

Now, looking at your past, can you see any misconceptions that you developed that may be thwarting your relational success? Are there aspects of your Personal Filter that might be pushing you toward one type of relationship that is unhealthy? For example, you do not have to repeat abusive relationships of any sort, or relationships that involve addictions (whether sex, drugs, alcohol, or food). Knowledge is power; sometimes just knowing what is hurting you can help you to let go of it.

On a lighter side, we also need to review the promises or decisions we made when we were younger regarding our hopes and dreams for relationships. We look at young people today and don't trust them to order a sandwich for us, yet we continue to live our lives by the vows we made at their young age! Did you decide in your heart when you were twelve that you would only date someone who looks likes James Spader? Did you take a blood oath and promise yourself to grunge music and plaid forever? These ideas served us well when we were first trying, but now it's time to know when to hold 'em and know when to fold 'em. For example, if you decided when you were sixteen that you would only marry a doctor, and you're now forty-two and still single, it may be time to ditch that promise to your Personal Filter.

See how you have grown from your past: have you changed for the better or for the worse in the following categories compared to when you were younger? You can judge against your high school, college, or young-adult self. Pick a period of time when you were dating the most—this can happen at different times or life stages for each of us. Give yourself one point for every improvement and two points for every change for the worse.

CATEGORY	BETTER	WORSE
Your face	1	2
Your body	1	2
Intelligence	1	2
Sense of humor, ability to make people laugh	1	2
Car	1	2
Job	1	2
People you live with	1	2
Home you live in	1	2
Recreation	1	2
Friends	1	2

YOUR SCORE

1-12	*Revel in Your Personal Filter*
13-16	*Tweak Your Personal Filter*
17-20	*Total Makeover*

REVEL IN YOUR PERSONAL FILTER

If you scored 12 points or less on this quiz then you should be congratulated. It's great to see that we really do improve with age, even if it's only been a few years. However, don't take your personal success too much to heart. The positive changes you've been able to make are terrific, but you need to make sure that your Personal Filter has also matured in the right proportions. The biggest temptation in attaining positive personal growth is to be conceited about your success, and begin to think so highly of yourself that you are stuck in dating denial.

In the Rating Game, recognizing that you've pulled yourself up in the world means a lot, but it's not going to necessarily get you a higher score. If you have had some great improvements since you were young then relish them, but don't idolize them. Don't think that your improvements mean you have arrived and now deserve the very best life has to offer. You certainly deserve what is best for you, and where you are right now. And in this game, that would be someone who rates exactly the same as you.

A second concern when you've experienced great personal improvement is to have dysmorphia. "Dysmorphia" is a psychological term for what occurs when you don't see yourself the way you are now. You may still be seeing that girl you used to be, in that awkward stage of puberty when you had braces and pimples. Or you may live as though you were the girl whose parents took care of everything, so you are not responsible for yourself. For better or for worse, you are no longer in that situation, so you are no longer that person. It's time to recognize who you are and own the accomplishments you've attained.

TWEAK YOUR PERSONAL FILTER

If you scored 13 to 16 points, it might be time to update your Personal Filter. You have shown that over time, some things about yourself have gotten better, while others have gotten worse. Join the club. Most of us have changed for the better, changed for the worse, or are sorting through the good and the bad.

But like so many things in life, if you can freshen up your Personal Filter then you'll be better off. I know that there is a strong temptation to keep your goals constant, as in "if it's not broken then don't fix it." But really, if you need help dating, then your Personal Filter might in fact be just the thing that's broken. Like the positive changes you've made in your life, little updates here and there are going to help you increase your score so that you can get to the best range of guys that will be right for you.

Tweaking your Personal Filter is not about making changes to yourself, but instead, it is about recognizing the changes that you have gone through and getting clarity on the real you right now. Maybe you were the cheerleader with the hot bod and not a lot to say in high school. Maybe you have changed and now you've got an average bod and a wealth of wisdom to share. So you need to tweak the way you look at yourself, so that you can see all that you have to offer, and reflect a more positive attitude out in the world. You don't have to be the person you once were, and rarely do we have it all at the same time. So be thankful for your newfound strengths, and know that there is a guy out there who will be a perfect match for you.

TOTAL MAKEOVER

If you scored 17 to 20 points, then you are in need of a whole new attitude and perhaps a clean hanky. The hanky will come in handy as you wave goodbye to yesterday and the Personal Filter that reflected how fantastic you were back then. You may currently believe that your best days are behind you, and this concept may be hurtful, or worse, holding you back from fully living your life right now. Your youth, whether or not it was perfect, can be a hard thing to let go of. We say something is nostalgic if it reminds us of times gone by, but the term really comes from an old medical disorder: there was once a real clinical diagnosis called nostalgia, which was given to mentally ill patients who could not let go of the past. We all resist change, and there is a strong temptation to stay the same, especially if we believe that things were great in the past. But I know that if you want to move forward with your life, nostalgia has to be put back on the shelf, at least for a little while.

The reality is that you will have better days in front of you, especially if you are wallowing in self-pity. By taking on a new attitude now, you'll break out of the dating rut you are in, and start looking forward to a new, better day. The first step will be to let go of this aspect of your Personal Filter. Look at your negative answers to the questions, and ask yourself if you feel hurt or resentful about answering negatively. Take a minute to validate that hurt, and then say the following, "I'm putting my past behind me so that I can make a fresh start. I can achieve the best that I can be." Release the anger attached to having to answer negatively, and repeat again down the list. By the end, you'll feel like you can do or be anything you want. The future is now an open door for you.

STEP TWO: DISCOVERING YOUR PRESENT

Now let's see how you perceive relative values right now. This exercise helps you decipher how you will score others on a scale of high, low, and average in each area by creating benchmarks for assigning the numbers. These questions are designed to stretch your thinking about the range of high to low to average, which will help set your Personal Filter range.

High, Low, and Average

Respond to the following as truthfully as possible. First, find the highest value that answers the questions:

1. Who is the best-looking actress of all time?
2. Name your favorite female movie character
3. Where is the best place to live on earth?

The following answers will determine your thoughts about "low":

1. Describe a homeless person
2. Name an evil dictator
3. Name a prison

Now, these responses will determine your thoughts about "average":

1. What do most people look like in your neighborhood?
2. What do you do on a typical Sunday?
3. Name a national chain restaurant

This quiz will help you set up benchmarks for your rating scale. Keep these values in the back of your mind while rating yourself, and rating men. The first part in each group will give you adjectives to assign as 1 (the worst) or 10 (the best) for face and body benchmarks. The second does the same for personality benchmarks. The last one in each category refers to the way you perceive life situation benchmarks.

STEP THREE: LOOKING TOWARD THE FUTURE

The final step is to be able to visualize your goals for the future. Sometimes our goals revolve around monotonous day-to-day needs (I need a new car) instead of exploring your hopes and dreams (I want to move to California). This exercise can help you gain clarity over what you truly yearn for. Knowing this will help you set your ideals and goals in dating. It is not that you have to achieve your ideal but knowing how you or a potential date compares to your ideal will help you set your Personal Filter.

The Fifty-Million-Dollar Day

Imagine that you had fifty million dollars left after having given your friends and family new homes, traveled the world, stuffed your closets, and thrown dozens of parties. How would you spend a perfect day? Think of what type of person you would like to spend this vast amount of time with, and what they would have to do to make you happy. Would you be happy if you were alone, or do you need the support of others? Now, take a piece of paper and write down exactly what you would do on your perfect day, hour by hour.

Why not work toward your real dream, starting today? It really doesn't matter if you don't have it all right now. By identifying what you want, you're taking the first important step.

Michelle

Michelle's family thinks she's too picky. Even though she dates often, she rarely settles into a relationship. Michelle works at a posh hotel as an event planner. She spends a lot of her day on the phone, and when she comes face-to-face with blushing brides, bridegrooms, corporate accountants, and celebrity management she is always 100 percent on. Michelle frequently emcees events for corporate clients, bringing all of her beauty, wit, and sophistication to the occasion. And for celebrity management she offers the height of discretion at the hotel, but never fails to have plenty of juicy stories for her girlfriends.

Michelle's family is small-town conservative even though they live in a medium-sized city. She recently met Drew, a local designer who shares her eclectic taste in music and art. They seem to get along, especially when they go to concerts and art shows. Drew is tall and has a nice face, but Michelle thinks he lacks a certain something. However, Michelle's older sister disagrees. Michelle's sister is married to a very nice man. Michelle knows that Drew is a good guy who would do anything for her, and would probably spend his life trying to make her happy. But no matter how hard she tries, she can't muster up real enthusiasm for him. Now Michelle feels guilty for dating Drew, even though the rest of the family is crazy about him. She continues to listen to her sister and keeps the relationship going, but she knows that she will eventually break Drew's heart and move on.

Dating a particular man because someone else thinks you should is like laughing because someone else thinks a joke is funny. You have to learn to trust your judgment and your Personal Filter. In this instance, Michelle knew all along that she and Drew didn't match up, but she stuck with him to make her family happy.

JUDGING OTHERS VERSUS BEING JUDGMENTAL

The Rating Game helps you weed out the men who are definitely not right for you, and by using your Personal Filter you will know which men to say no to. This statement can sound kind of judgmental, and that's because it is. You may think that judging people is so junior high school. In fact, I believe that we must judge people. The Rating Game is all about judging people. However, I'm not talking about judging people in a mean-spirited, all-or-nothing way. The point is to judge men to see if they are a match for you in a romantic relationship, not to see if they have value to the rest of the world. As the great Dr. Martin Luther King, Jr., said, "I have a dream, that my four little children will one day live in a nation where they will not be judged by the color of their skin but by the content of their character."

There is nothing wrong with judging someone based on their character. Determining how someone presents themselves, how they take care of themselves, and what they've done with their life is an honorable assessment. However, there are some judgments that are considered immoral by even the most finicky daters:

- Judging people based on the color of their eyes or the color of their skin is not fair; judging people on what they like to look at is fair.

- Judging people based on what they like to eat is unwarranted; judging people based on what they say is warranted.

- Judging people based on how much money their family has is not fair; judging people based on what they like to buy is fair.

- Judging should be a character thing.

ARE SOME PEOPLE *REALLY* BETTER THAN OTHERS?

In the dating world, the answer is a resounding yes. Our current cultural mind-set does not want you to believe that someone could be "better" than others, or even better than you. People especially do not want you to think that you could be better than them. However, some people are better *for* you than others, and identifying these characteristics is actually a positive tool for creating a dating life.

When we are out with the girls we like to think that we are the best; if a relationship didn't work out for one of your friends it's because the guy she was dating wasn't good enough. While this attitude might make you popular among your girlfriends it is not always true. You might not want to be the bearer of bad news for your BFF, but when you are evaluating your own relationship, it is best to be honest. If you can get to a place where you can handle the truth about yourself and the men you have dated, then the next time you put yourself out in the dating world you are more likely to get what you really want. You can—and should—judge if any particular man is good enough for you.

The concept of certain people being better than others was a societal norm until the 1960s. Then the rhetoric of "we are all good" and "don't judge me" took root shortly after the civil rights and women's liberation movements. All of a sudden everyone was as good as everyone else. Self-improvement books were filling the shelves, and people were willing to pay any price just to feel better about themselves.

So from all of our self-exploration we have learned that there is no point in judging people based on where they came from, how much money their parents had, or by the color of their skin. None of these attributes reveal a person's true character, personality, or beauty. And you can find every type of beauty, body type, personality, and life situation in every color. In fact, I believe that judging someone's personality or life situation based on their skin color is one of the worst mistakes that can be made.

Unfortunately, we all have racial stereotypes to contend with. I was raised in an interracial home and still make quick judgments. That doesn't make me a monster for having these thoughts, but I'm not proud of them. The key is to not hang on to racial stereotypes when they surface, and certainly to not use any sort of ethnic stereotype as a basis for making dating judgments. I know I can describe the way someone looks by envoking race, but after that, I know that there really isn't anything more to say.

You will have a better chance of being attracted to someone— and being found attractive by someone—if you are not indulging in stereotypes. Better still, approach dating with a wide-open worldview. I have seen it firsthand in my travels in the past few years, that no matter where I go I find that there are more similarities among the human race than differences. I have eaten crawfish with cajuns in a bayou; sipped cucumber martinis at Chateau Marmont with movie stars and the film industry elite; canoed down the Amazon basin with tribal men from the jungles of Ecuador; partied in the south of France; road tripped Ethiopia in a Land Cruiser; dipped my feet in the Bahamas' blue waters with government officials; and seen the Blue Mountains of Jamaica with the Rastafarians. The one thing I have learned in all my travels is that there is always a range of men and if you recognize your range and learn to keep your options open, you will never be far from an eligible, datable guy.

If you think that you are not attracted to a certain race ask yourself the question, "How many people do I really know who represent this race?" A more expanding answer is, "I haven't been attracted to anyone from that race *yet*." That keeps your options open to the bazillions of people you have never met and keeps you from making racial decisions in your rating.

Judging people based on the wealth of their family is as presumptuous and pretentious as judging someone by their skin color. Rich kids can be successful or flops. They can also be nice or mean, endearing, or even buffoons. A poor child can succeed, and a rich kid can hit skid row. The Forbes Fortune 500 list is full of rags-to-riches billionaire stories. Just because a person's parents have money does not determine what his life will be like. Sometimes money can ruin a person. It's better to judge a person based on what he does with the opportunities that he has, instead of the opportunities that he has been given because of wealth.

Judging people by their origin is tricky, and there are many people who are trapped in the stigma of where they came from. It is a typical human trait to make assumptions about a person when given just a little information. But when we assume that one person is like someone else because he is from the same place, we box people in and do not give them a chance to be an individual. Worse, we are then left focusing on the hype instead of the truth.

Even though people from the same place may eat the same thing, live in a similar manner, or have similar faith or customs, it does not mean that their personalities are the same. It does not mean that they have the same drive or sense of humor. What it could mean is that they have adapted to their circumstance in the same way as others that live in the same region. If you put any one ethnic group in a different environment they would probably adapt to their new situation in the same way as the people originally from that region. For example, people who grew up on farms are thought to be hearty; but what about all the ones who left that lifestyle behind and moved to the city? Soon that ole' farmer might start eating sushi and practicing for the Tour de France on the weekends. People change when you change their surroundings.

The point here is that as we move forward into the Rating Game, it is impossible to rate without judging others. But the key is not to become judgmental. Rating someone lower or higher than you simply means that this particular person isn't right for you. That doesn't make them a bad person; it just makes them a bad match. So make sure that you keep your judgments to yourself, no matter how right you think you are.

YOUR PERSONAL FILTER GUIDES YOU TOWARD COMPATIBILITY

Everyone has their own perception of themselves as well as the way they fit into the world. If you created a Web site where you posted your picture and address and let other people match you with potential dates, the matches would likely be far off base from what you would choose for yourself. That's because everyone else would be matching you based on their perception of the four categories. They would be matching you on who they think you are or who they think you should be with. With only a picture to go by, they would try and match you solely based on your race, or on the preconceived notions they have about your look or address.

For example, others may look at my picture and think that because I live in Hollywood, I would be interested in guys who are fast and flashy. Because my skin is dark, some might think I was looking to meet a basketball player. Or, if I sent in a picture of myself wearing a business suit, some might pair me with a banker. However, I know that I'm not interested in any of these types of men. I know my Personal Filter, and I'm looking for a man who meets my needs based on what I've learned about my past, present, and what I want for the future.

Drawing on your Personal Filter ensures that your needs are taken into consideration during the Rating Game. The point of the game is not to date just anyone, but to find men in your range who are going to be compatible with you. They need to meet your basic requirements based on the things you like about yourself, on the scale you will create ranging from high to low, and how they may fit into your future.

Remembering your Personal Filter is like learning the rules of the road for driving. You know that every time you get in the car, you must remember what you learned in driver's education—that you can't cross the yellow line in the middle of the road and that a red octagon always means stop. You've learned which side of the road to drive on and how many car lengths it takes to stop at ten, twenty, and thirty miles per hour. You've internalized these rules over the years and now you can get into a car and start driving. It's not that you aren't focusing on the rules, you know them by heart, and now you can focus on the enjoyment of the drive, the music, and maybe even the company in your passenger seat.

The way you will use your Personal Filter is very much the same. You learned about your style and what you value. You discovered ways to express your highs, lows, and averages based on what you value, and you set goals for the future. When you rate men, and rate yourself, you'll find that you automatically call on this knowledge to help you make decisions. But just like that yellow stripe that divides the road, your Personal Filter will always be there for you, setting your internal boundaries, and helping you decide who you are truly compatible with.

3.

Where Do I Rate?

A healthy happiness comes from knowing
that what you have to offer is enough for someone else,
and knowing that what someone else has to offer
is enough for you.

—REBA

IN THE PAST few decades, our society has moved into a major "feel good" mode. Everyone has become special just because they exist. We've renamed jobs: secretaries are now called administrative assistants, and garbage men are sanitation engineers. Even doctors are more special—now they're cardiologists, plastic surgeons, urologists, and primary care providers. And while some of this global pat on the back has done a world of good—African American children no longer grow up feeling inferior because of the color of their skin, and mean-spirited terms such as "midget" have been eradicated—the downside is that we've taken the "feel good" concept a couple of steps too far. Now every kid gets a thumbs-up even if their work is subpar and every team has to win no matter how badly it plays.

At the same time, we've embraced perfection as the mediocre standard. Our society has created ideals that are totally unattainable. Twenty years ago the average American woman strived to wear a size six; now, if you can't fit into a zero or two you sign up for Weight Watchers. Many models and actresses suffer from anorexia in order to maintain their body, have plastic surgery to get the face they want, and still need to be airbrushed for their magazine spreads. We have been trained to think that even with minimal effort we should be able to achieve perfection.

Brad Pitt said it best when he was playing Tyler Durden in the popular movie *Fight Club*. His line was, "We've all been raised on television to believe that one day we'd all be millionaires, and movie gods, and rock stars. But we won't. And we're slowly learning that fact. And we're very, very pissed off."

We fall into the same trap of searching for perfection in many different aspects of our lives. Besides constantly dwelling on our looks, many of us pine over the biggest house with professional-grade kitchens, the fanciest cars loaded with the latest technologies, and take bragging rights with window stickers displaying our alma maters. There is nothing wrong with being technosexual, but our toys and awards should not define us. Nor should we all think that we are entitled to everything at the Mac store. All of this desperate wanting to show off your stuff leaves the "average" person feeling a lot less than average.

But when we get right down to it, we all are really only slightly better, or slightly worse, than average. And that's okay. You are probably never going to be a movie star. Chances are slim that a modeling agency will ring your bell because their scout saw you at

Starbucks. And that's why we start the Rating Game by taking a good hard look at ourselves. It's time to come to terms with the real you. Let's celebrate your unique talents, and recognize your failures.

CHECK IN WITH YOUR SELF-ESTEEM

I want you to formulate a realistic self-image, not judging yourself by the way your favorite celeb looks or by how happy the woman bouncing in the meadow in the ad for depression medication seems. Again, it's about taking a holistic look at yourself and realizing that the perfection you see in the media may be out of reach for you. Even though celebs appear perfect, they need a team of people and bloated hair-and-makeup budgets to achieve their distinctive looks. And those people in the medical ads, you've got to think that if their life is so perfect, why did they need the Zoloft in the first place? So before you can judge others, let's see if you have fallen prey to society's obsesssion with pills or the *Desperate Housewives* hype, either one of which can overinflate or deflate your self-esteem.

An unrealistic perception of yourself may be causing you to date people who will never be right for you. If you have low self-esteem, you might end up dating down. And if your high self-esteem doesn't match what you are really offering in the dating world, you'll find that you are dating up, or worse, not dating at all.

Everyone has moments of low self-esteem. I've heard it said that self-esteem stems from an internal belief of knowing that what we are doing or who we are being is right. If so, it makes sense that when we do something that we know is wrong or not good for us, our self-esteem suffers. It doesn't matter how many thumbs-up you get or how many times the ref calls it a tie. If you know that you did not do well in any aspect of your life, it will change the way you see yourself.

I suffered terribly from low self-esteem about my body when I was in college. I went to school in a beach community, and had put on the freshman fifteen all on my backside. I discovered this one spring day when I was trying on a bathing suit. I freaked out! I was unable to leave the dressing room. I called my BFF and he had to talk me out of my anxiety attack. My self-esteem took a double whammy. I felt terrible not only because I couldn't fit my big butt into a bikini, but also because I had to deal with the guilt of eating all that food I knew I should have avoided.

The sad fact of my life was that I lived next door to a doughnut shop! Say no more, right? I used those doughnuts to comfort me during all-night cram sessions, stressful test weeks, and lonely weekends and holidays without my family. Every time I would pop a warm chocolate morsel in my mouth I was happy, at least for the moment. That all ended when I caught a glimpse of my reflection in the window of the campus library. I was so mortified that I covered my enormous tushie with my backpack and made a beeline for my car.

It wasn't until I finished college that I was finally able to drop all the weight I had gained. One time my friend Atouzo came over for Thanksgiving dinner. We not only stuffed that turkey, we stuffed our tummies. The next day we faced our guilt head-on and we learned something about ourselves. We figured out that if we ran really slow we could run for a solid mile. This concept changed my life, and I started exercising regularly.

Then I started surfing. I loved the freeing feeling of being covered from ankle to neck in a black wet suit. I'd always loved the water but was intimidated by the ocean waves. Each time I went out I felt like I was facing my fears. Needless to say, as my weight dropped and my surfing improved, my self-esteem soared. Within months I was in the best shape of my life. It was hard work, but I did the right thing and I felt good about myself for that.

My physical transformation was accompanied by big changes to my social life. At first I really did experience that much-sought-after moment of glory: I knew that I looked hot and it was clear that men were attracted to me more than ever before. While this sounds like every woman's dream, it was actually not so easy to deal with. I knew that parts of me had changed, but parts of me had stayed the same. I still had flaws and situations to deal with that I did not think my new class of suitors would appreciate.

At first I met several amazingly good-looking men who seemed to have everything going for them. But even though I looked the part, I had to try really hard to fit in with them. I wasn't really being true to myself, because their lives were vastly different than mine. It is disheartening to have gorgeous men attracted to you knowing that your lifestyle can't sustain their affection.

One night a girlfriend and I were able to get away to have a cocktail at a trendy lounge overlooking a pool at a swanky hotel. We could only stay for one drink as I had finagled a very short-term babysitter—my girlfriend's hubby wanted her home soon. But I found myself talking to the most beautiful man I had ever seen. My friend sat astonished beside me. In a few moments I learned that this former Calvin Klein model was interested in dating me.

We exchanged numbers and the next day he invited me back to the pool to hang out. I was thrilled that he called, but knew my domestic life on the sleepy side of town would not mesh with his up-and-coming lifestyle. I got so frustrated that I went back to my old ways, looking for someone who loved me for my weaknesses instead of my assets. It would take another wedding dress before the Rating Game would help me sort out how my strengths and weaknesses work together.

GIVE YOURSELF THE PROPS YOU DESERVE

The Rating Game gives you a chance to finally see how your assets balance out your flaws. There are four areas that our attributes fall into and to which equal consideration is given. I truly believe that every woman has wonderful traits—they just need to be uncovered. So give yourself the props you deserve, wherever you deserve them.

The key is to be realistic about yourself so that you can rate your four areas—face, body, personality, and life situation—correctly. If you are suffering from an overall low self-esteem, it is probably because you are overly focused on a negative area. Similarly, if you have an overinflated self-image it is most likely because you are focusing on a strength in one area. You don't want to overinflate your score by omitting any of the areas, otherwise you could turn into a pumpkin at Cinderella's ball.

I have a pretty good idea about my score, and usually I'm fine with the results. But I know that about once a year I'm able to pull off a really high score. For example, a few years ago I was invited to attend the opening night of the musical *Hairspray*. I wore a fabulous strapless dress that clung to my new, well-shaped bod. A long red carpet led us from the show to the afterparty. Ricki Lake from the original film was there, as well as lots of other celebrities. I went with a good friend who is a bit older than me and extremely handsome—that Date #2 comes in handy! When we got to the party we ended up at a cocktail table next to a couple of guys from a television entertainment show. The four of us started dancing, and out of the corner of my eye I noticed that a bearded John Stamos was looking at me from a table nearby. I knew I looked hot: I was toned, tan, and was dancing with three guys who all looked like network executives. I was thrilled to have gotten his attention at all, because I consider him to be one of the hottest men alive. That night I knew that I had faked a nine, but like Cinderella I knew that come midnight, I would be a 7.75 again. I was able to reach a 9 because I was just a girl dancing at a party. In my best dress on my best day I appeared to be a 9 from across the room, but given even a three-minute conversation anyone would be able to tell that I wasn't hitting all 9s across the board. This level of scrutiny is easier said than done. Without knowing how to run the numbers it can be almost impossible.

Michael

Michael had made a lot of money in the dot-com craze back in the late nineties, but when it went bust he moved in with his parents, and at thirty-two is now living in their basement. He told me he has done everything he could think of to start dating again, but that he has terrible luck with women. Everything? I thought. I had to know where he went wrong.

I probed Michael and his very gabby sister and I found out that when he was in high school, Michael resented the fact that looks mattered so much with the girls around him. He rebelled by ignoring the slight pudge on his average frame. He did little with his thin brown hair, and did not pay attention to his wardrobe. His slightly acerbic personality didn't enhance his ability to socialize. Michael knew that he wasn't a whiz kid, but found a niche with computers and spent much of his adolescence behind his PC. He stuck mostly to himself at his state university and was happy to graduate with a software engineering degree where he was surrounded by guys just like him for four straight years.

After landing an entry-level position at a Fortune 500, Michael actually made a friend, and the two started a distribution line on the Internet. Within months the word of their progressive idea spread and investors started to pour money into their accounts. Seemingly overnight, Michael had a promising business and a Porsche. Best of all, Michael felt like a new man. So much so that he assumed that his career success had changed him into a hot commodity in the dating world. Sure, he turned some heads in his new canary-yellow Carrera GT, and with his extroverted business partner by his side he could even approach pretty women.

Even with all his monetary success, Michael had only changed one area of his life. His life situation had changed but not his body, face, or personality. He was expecting to attract girls in a higher range because of his higher life situation. He thought he could meet their needs, and he also hoped that he could hook them in so they could meet his. But as he learned, he had subconsciously overrated himself, and once his money was gone, he wasn't able to get past a first drink with a beautiful woman.

RATING YOURSELF

You are now going to evaluate every aspect of yourself in a very methodical manner. The categories are divided into four basic areas: face, body, personality, and life situation. The first two categories are immediate and visual. The second two will help you define the depth of your character. In the end, you'll find that you are the sum of these four categories. *People know you by your face, you access the world with your body, you express yourself with your personality, and live within the structure of your life situation.*

In order to get a full picture of who we are, we're going to highlight our good points, and come to terms with the bad. We'll put our weaknesses on the table and then temper them with our strengths. As you evaluate each area, you'll come up with a composite number. This number will give you a sense of how the rest of the world views you, as well as a better sense on how you perceive your worth.

Read through the category descriptions as well as the definitions of what each number means. Later, you'll use these same standards to help you rate others. Though it can be scary at first, most people are very pleased with their final scores. That's because you will make the decision of how you rate based on your Personal Filter, which I define as your particular expectations about your life. Recognize that each of us has different ideals for what is considered to be a high score or a low score. When you are playing the Rating Game, other people's opinions do not matter in the least. You will determine what the very best value is for you in each of the categories.

For example, if being a business professional is your ideal for perfection, then you need to see if you are living up to your expectations for this type of person in each of the four areas. This would include how you look in the office, how you wear your hair and makeup (face), how you dress (body), how you act around others (personality), and how well you are achieving this lifestyle, including what you drive, where you have gone to school, and where you live now, as well as other lifestyle choices (life situation).

You will start by identifying what your ideal of perfection is for this person, and then determine how close or far you are from that ideal. The following definitions of each of the numbers will help you determine how you actually rate.

UNDERSTANDING THE NUMBERS

Am I going to be a 7 or an 8?
What if I'm a 3? I'll hide in a closet and never come out again!

If the idea of rating yourself is giving you an arithmetic anxiety attack, relax. You're likely to have a higher rating than you currently imagine. Remember, your rating is an average of all four categories, specifically based on what you alone think. So, even if you score low in one category, there are three others that will reflect your redeeming qualities, which will help to increase your rating.

The number of points you'll dole out will also be unique to you.

Some women are very liberal in assigning points, while others are harder on themselves and skimp on the numbers. The way you give numbers is part of your Personal Filter and does factor into your measuring technique.

Below are the numbers and what they generally represent. By the end of this book you will have each of these definitions memorized and be able to shoot them out like bullets in the Clint Eastwood movie *The Good, the Bad, and the Ugly.* While you will decide what qualities each number will represent, there are some constants: 10 will always be the highest number, 1 will always be the lowest, and 5 will always be the average. Because 10s and 1s are the very best and very worst, you'll dole out very few of them—perfection and disasters don't happen very often.

When you rate yourself, I suggest that you give yourself a break. That's why I usually start at 5 as the base, and then determine if I'm worth a few more points on the way up to 10. If things aren't looking so good, then I start with 5 and work my way down toward 1.

10 = PERFECTION

9 = THE BEST IN THE ROOM

8 = GREAT

7 = GOOD

6 = ABOVE AVERAGE

5 = AVERAGE

4 = OKAY

3 = BELOW AVERAGE

2 = NOT GOOD

1 = CALL SECURITY

I = CALL SECURITY

When we rate a 1 that means that there is little redeeming quality in that area. A 1 face will be very difficult to look at. A 1 body will be severely deformed. A 1 for personality will be comatose or a violent criminal. Similarly, a 1 in a life situation will equal incarceration or a hospice. If none of these situations apply to you, skip ahead and start at 2.

2 = NOT GOOD

A 2 rating is like getting a thumbs-down in any area of your life. Scoring a 2 is like getting an F on your report card. A 2 face may be scarred. A 2 body will be morbidly obese. A 2 for personality will be given if you are desperately shy. And a 2 in life situation will mean that you are still living with your mother, and liking it.

3 = BELOW AVERAGE

The 3 score in an area can be thought of as the "best" of the low numbers. This means that a 3 is the last number that has an inherent negative connotation. It is barely low. A 3 score for your face would be appropriate if you have bad hygiene. A 3 body will seriously need to hit the gym. A 3 personality might find themselves alone all the time. Similarly, a 3 in life situation would be reasonable if you are stuck in a dead-end job.

4 = OKAY

4 is when the ratings start to get positive. A 4 is a hearty "not bad." A 4 is like saying that you have nothing to worry about. Amaz-

ingly, many women I meet are fine with being a 4. A 4 is like getting a C on your report card, a grade that says that no matter what,
we are not failing. It is like a general admission ticket that says,
"We made it!"

5 = AVERAGE

Average is not a dirty word. In fact, in the Rating Game, a 5 is a
solid number and there is nothing wrong with that. Average is
where most people are at. The fact is, 5s have the most fun because
there are more of them. This middle marker is a great litmus test.
To find out what a 5 means in any area just ask this question,
"What do most people look like in this area?" Some would call it
"grading on the curve." A 5 face is pleasant and nonthreatening. A
5 body could stand to lose a few pounds, but is probably just fine.
A 5 for personality is easy to be with and not too demanding. Similarly, a 5 in life situation is best described as "steady" in every aspect of life.

6 = ABOVE AVERAGE

The 6 rating is almost a gray area. A 6 is a solid B, not better, not
worse. It is a face that is better-than-average but not good-looking;
a body that is better than the average person but not impressive; a
personality or life situation that is above average but not inspiring.

7 = GOOD

This number is well above average and represents qualities that are
straight-up positive. A 7 is high-quality. A face that is a 7 would be

considered good-looking. A 7 body would be select. Give yourself a 7 for personality if you know that people are drawn to you. As a life situation, think about rating yourself a 7 if you are content with what you've got.

8 = GREAT

Once you get to great there is no more debate! An 8 in any area is excellent. An eight is like getting an A on your report card. It is above and beyond average in every way. An 8 face is extremely beautiful. An 8 body is athletic in every sense of the word. An 8 personality is effervescent. Whatever qualities you deem amazing are the qualities you need to assign an 8. An 8 in life situation would be a job that is on the fast track in a career that you love.

9 = THE BEST IN THE ROOM

If an 8 is an A on a report card then a 9 is an A+. A 9 is staggeringly brilliant. A 9 is the best that most will ever see. There are very few people who score an overall 9, and for those that live outside of major urban areas, such as Los Angeles, New York, or Paris, you might find that it is lonely at the top. However, there are many who have this marvelous rating in one area or another. A mind-blowing face, an astonishing body, a personality like the Pied Piper, or a life situation that is absolutely fabulous.

10 = PERFECTION

Perfection is very rare. Swimsuit models can get 10s for body or sometimes face, but it is almost unheard of for someone to get a 10 in all areas. Perfection is unnatural and almost unattainable, so bear that in mind when bestowing yourself with a 10.

Danielle

Dani had every reason to lavish high points on herself. With blond hair and blue eyes, the only thing cuter than her face was her shining personality. Danielle had an exciting job that required her to travel with the hottest bands. Oh, did I mention a hot body, too? So, what did Danielle rate herself? A 4 in all categories! I was shocked. Was this all about her low self-esteem? No way—Danielle was just a hard marker who was bent on holding others to the same standards she set for herself. However, she gave points to boys she was with in the same way. So a 4 for Dani is like an 8 to others, but it all evens out in her world.

THE CATEGORIES

Now let's review each of the categories, and see the different components that fall within their range. Read the definitions for each category. In the end you'll know if your face, body, personality, or life situation is below average, above average, perfection, or anywhere in between.

FACE

Face is our first category because faces are the first thing we look at. It's the first thing we check in the mirror every morning and many of us continue to check it out all day. Can you walk past a reflective surface, let alone a mirror, without slowing down and giving yourself a once-over? Don't tell me that you've never looked at your reflection in a store window, a toaster, or your car's rearview mirror? You've never discreetly checked your lipstick in the back of a butter knife at a restaurant when your date wasn't looking? It's not vanity that drives us to do this continual head-bobbing. Our faces identify us. They communicate who we are, what we're feeling, and many times, how we feel about ourselves.

So how do you rate a face—especially when it's yours? Is there a way to define what is beautiful? When rating your own face, you're more likely to start counting freckles and large pores and deducting points left and right. Stop it! That's not what this exercise is about. Instead, you can accurately rate your face positively if your skin has a healthy color and glow. Nothing is more appealing than a face that is well taken care of. Are there oily patches? Is the skin dry or chapped? Is it blemished or scarred? Are there wrinkles? These would all be considerations where you may want to lower your face score by a point.

If you have any questions about how good-looking you may be, try this exercise:

Pull your hair back off your face and look into a mirror. What we're looking for is symmetry, meaning balance and proportion. Models' faces, statues of gods and goddesses, and portraits of beautiful people all have symmetry. Features are evenly spaced and in proportion to one another. Horizontally, the face is divided into thirds. The top line is where the eyes are set. The bottom line is where the lips are. Between those two lines is the nose, with the vertical line going down the center of the nose. The more symmetrical your face is the better-looking you are. If the eyes are too close together or too far apart, if the nose is out of line, or if the mouth is crooked, the symmetry is off.

Next, consider what's on this face of yours. Start with your hair. Your hair should not only frame the face, it should accentuate it. Consider if the style is complementary to your personality and your lifestyle. Is it up-to-date? Is it clean? Is it touchable? Start with average and rate your hair and face together. Are you a 5–5 (5 face, 5 hair), or a 6–7? Next, see what's up with the rest of your features, and rate them as well. Take off a point for facial hair. Add a point for a nice smile, especially if your teeth are clean and cared for.

Finally, consider the message you are sending with your facial body language. Our faces are constantly sending out messages, telling others what's going on inside our heads, including how we feel about ourselves. Consider if your face is sending a positive or negative message.

BODY

Women have always felt pressure about how their bodies look. So much focus has been placed on how we should look that breast augmentations and eating disorders are now completely commonplace, especially in L.A., where I live. You can't disregard that men are drawn to female beauty, but we should never assume that any woman is defined solely by her body: remember, one attribute does not a woman make.

When rating your body, there is more to consider than six-pack abs or love handles. Take the following criteria into consideration for coming up with your rating.

Grooming. Personal cleanliness is a must. Are your fingernails manicured or at least cleaned and clipped? What about body odor, uncontrolled perspiration, stinky feet, bad breath?

Attire. Clothing doesn't have to sport designer logos but it does have to be clean, unwrinkled, fit well, and be appropriate to the occasion. If you need a massive wardrobe overhaul, take off a point.

Physique. Tall, short, skinny, or fat. Muscle-bound or lean. Apple shape or pear shape. Safe to say, there are more body types than there are jeans to put them in. But for the sake of setting a constant on the scale, the top spots belong to a healthy and strong body that is well-proportioned in height and weight. The bottom of the scale is an unhealthy body (thin may be in, but anorexic doesn't win points).

Body language. Your body language can communicate just as much information as your face. Consider posture: do you stand up straight with your shoulders back or slouching and dragging your feet? Are you compensating for being too tall by hunching over? Arms and legs that are crossed are defensive signs and keep people away. Looking down and not maintaining eye contact shows insecurity.

PERSONALITY

The trick here is to be able to identify the person you really are. What follows is a series of opposite traits and characteristics. Use this list to get your mind thinking about which personality traits you value. Then decide how you rate your personality by seeing which apply to you.

- Supportive, encouraging, a can-do spirit, or a nothing-ever-goes-right attitude, hopeless, or fearful

- Friendly, warm, someone who likes people, or a loner who avoids social situations

- Laughs easily, sometimes, or not at all

- Caring, compassionate, and considerate, or apathetic, doesn't want to get involved

- Cool, level-headed problem solver, or quick to anger, gets upset easily, mopes, whines, and blames others

- Ambitious and passionate, or content to do little

- Outgoing, gregarious, talkative, or quiet, shy, cautious

- Trusting of self and others, or suspicious, envious, jealous

- Confident, or full of self-doubt

- Well-mannered, respectful, or brash, rude, overbearing

- Generous, helpful, or selfish, cheap

- Leader, or follower

- Active, outgoing, or restrained, low energy

- Focused, or scattered

LIFE SITUATION

The life situation category is composed of the individual facets of your life. The areas to take into consideration are listed below. Feel free to add to this list according to what is currently going on in your own life situation. Then, see how your life stacks up to what you think is ideal. By rating your life situation, you'll be able to determine how content you are right now. For example, if you have always wanted a large social circle but don't have any friends you will probably score lower. Using the 1 to 10 scale, rate how happy you are with your:

Health. Do you have any chronic health problems that are holding you back in any way? Do you take care of yourself? Do you have health insurance?

Career. Employed? Full time? Part time? Self-employed? Does your job take you away from home? Salary? Job security?

Finances. How do you handle money? Is there a mortgage, car payment, child support, student loans, credit card debt?

Housing. Do you own or rent your home? Do you live alone? With a roommate?

Intelligence. Level of education completed (high school, GED, some college, college degree)?

Interests/hobbies. What do you do after work? Athlete or fan? Any hobbies? Do you collect anything? Do you spend enough time pursuing your interests?

Friends. Do you have a lot of friends? Close friends? Friends of the opposite sex? Do you spend enough time with your friends?

Spirituality. Are you connected with God? Are you a practicing member of a particular religion or a lapsed follower?

Vices. Do you smoke, do drugs, gamble?

Pets. Do you have any? Do you like animals?

GUESS WHO'S BETTER THAN YOU?

Still don't think people can be better than you? Just take a look at this list. These are the absolute 10s in each category. None have 10s in every area but have at least one area locked down. Now see how you stack up.

Face
- Wrinkle cream spokesmodels
- All of Tom Brady's girlfriends
- Your five-year-old niece

Body

- Brazilian swimsuit models
- High school girls in gym shorts
- Beach volleyball players

Personality

- Mother Teresa
- Meredith Viera
- Kelly Ripa

Life Situation

- Soon-to-be-princess Kate Middleton
- Harry Potter author, J. K. Rowling
- Melinda Gates

DO THE MATH

Plug in the numbers from the four categories in the pyramid that follows. First, look at them just as they are. Do they represent how you really feel about each aspect of yourself? Are they relatively in the same range, or are there certain numbers that are much higher, or much lower than the rest? The high numbers are called spikes, the low ones are called dips. The spikes are your accomplishments: these are numbers that you celebrate! The dips, on the other hand, show you where your insecurities lie. See if you can glean any understanding about yourself when you look at your lowest numbers. Is there room for improvement in any of the categories? We'll look at that issue more closely in the next chapter.

The next step is to calculate your average score. Simply add all the points together and divide the total by four. This number is the final rating! While the other numbers represent different parts of you, the only number that is important now is your final rating. Knowing this should be enough to stop giving yourself such a hard time about any one facet of your life.

Don't forget the number definitions:

10 = PERFECTION

9 = THE BEST IN THE ROOM

8 = GREAT

7 = GOOD

6 = ABOVE AVERAGE

5 = AVERAGE

4=OKAY

3 = BELOW AVERAGE

2 = NOT GOOD

1 = CALL SECURITY

- Your face: _____
- Your body: _____
- Your personality: _____
- Your life situation: _____
  TOTAL: _____ ÷4 = _____ your score!

For example, if you scored a 6 for face, 5 for body, 7 for personality, and 4 for life situation, your final rating would be a 5.5. *Going forward, you are going to be looking for guys that rate exactly the same as you.* If, like in the following scenario, your final score contained a fractional answer, you should be dating to the lowest round number. In this case, you would be dating in the 5s.

Laura

Being the oldest sister in a family where depression keeps Dad from working is like walking around with an anvil on your shoulder. Knowing that everyone in the family was counting on her was almost too much for Laura to bear. Thankfully, her mom had a good job teaching at the local high school. However, having her mom work at Laura's school meant that she didn't get a break or a chance to be carefree all day. She told me, "From the time I got up in the morning I had to be cheery enough to balance Dad's melancholy. Then at school I had to be the perfect student as a role model for my sister and to prove that though my dad was sick the rest of the family was normal. By the time I got home it was all about being a counselor to Dad's depression and being a shoulder for Mom to lean on.

"I don't consider my upbringing a tragic one but I can see the ramifications of it in my adult life. My controlling nature often pushes people away. It's not that they hate me, it's just that I'm not the first person that gets called when there's something fun happening, so I often end up alone. My sister was always considered the one with the pretty face but I always had the dancer's body and a great personality, when I'm not obsessing over life's details.

"In life I do well. I am in a leadership group at my church and run a small study group that meets at my house. I have success in my career and in my finances. Unfortunately, my dating life has suffered. At twenty-five I had never even been kissed or had a real date. I felt like I was at the bottom of the dating pole until I rated myself. I gave myself a 4 for face, 6 for body, 7 for personality, and 6 for life situation. The numbers were tallied and I ended up a 5.75! I was so excited to be average. I had lived my whole life feeling like I was bottom rung in the world of relationships and now I'm finding out the whole time I'm at the same place as just about everybody else."

Soon Laura felt good enough about herself to get out into her local singles scene. She joined a gym, and while she was there she started talking to—and rating—the men she thought she was compatible with. It didn't take too long before she was meeting guys who were interested in her, and that she felt she was interested in.

WERE YOU DATING DOWN BECAUSE YOU DIDN'T LIKE YOURSELF?
While it's good to put the past behind us, there is a lesson we can learn from our previous dating mistakes. Soon you will be able to see if your numbers support what you may have already realized. Once you learn how to apply the numbers to men you will be able to think back to your last relationship and see if your score put you ahead or behind.

If you were dating down, chances are that you chose men who were comfortable to be around because you felt in some ways superior to them. Now that you can see your numbers, do they prove this point? Or, maybe your numbers will show you that you were choosing less favorable men because that was all you believed you deserved? Dating down doesn't mean that the person you were dating was bad, but it does mean that they were not right for you. By looking at your rating, you can see exactly what kind of guy you deserve.

Julia

Julia is a beautiful, twenty-year-old girl who has a bad life situation (3). She has a great body (8) and face (7) but lives with her immigrant parents in a small apartment on the wrong side of town. She has spent most of her life taking care of her sick grandmother and helping her mom clean houses for money. Julia has a cheerful personality when you meet her (I'd rank that a 6). She is creative and talented: she designs most of her own clothes in her tiny apartment. But she is always focused on the negative attributes of coming from the wrong side of town and having so many family responsibilities. Consequently Julia has dated down several times. Her typical guy is a thug, because she'd thought that was all she deserved. She also has a pattern of ending relationships before they even got started because she was so unsatisfied with the crude behavior of the boys she dated.

Julia saw herself based on her lowest qualities instead of based on her combined score. She simply neglected to factor in all her wonderful attributes. In her mind, Julia was only the woman who cleaned toilets and was embarrassed to have people to her house. Once I rated her and showed her that she was a 6, she was finally able to realize that she was so much more than her life situation score. The next time Julia went out, she had a little more spring in her step, and looked around for guys who more closely matched her better-than-average rating.

ARE YOU DATING UP OR ARE YOU REALLY *SO* HOT?

If your numbers prove what you knew all along, and you are an 8, 9, or (gasp!) 10, then you really are as hot as you think! Dang, girl! Get out there and find someone who is just as hot as you. But if the numbers showed that you were stretching your reach just a bit, you might want to let go of the stars. Dating up is tempting, no doubt about it. But trust me, these relationships won't work out for long.

Leslie

Leslie was a quiet but not calm middle child in a boisterous southern family. She is a very good-looking woman (8) with an attractive figure (7) but is extremely intense and socially awkward (3). Her sense of humor often gets trapped behind a piercing stare and limited facial expression. Worse, Leslie works around the clock as an attorney, so while she is well-paid, she has little time to party (4).

Even when she does have time to go out, dating has never been Leslie's forte. She is only attracted to extremely good-looking guys, and while they will ask her out, the dinner date never turns into much more. Yet she desperately hopes to find a long-term relationship with a stunning man.

Leslie was initially shocked when we ran her rating. Her score of 5.5 was clearly lower than the guys she was trying to reel in. If she keeps going for the handsome prince type, she will never find true love. Instead, she needs to cast a wider net, and find some-one who is more in her range. While she is hot and scores high in some areas, her awkward personality and limited availability score very low in personality and life situation. That's why her total score is just average.

I'M NOT DONE WITH YOU YET

You now have a good understanding about how the Rating Game works, including the categories to consider and the values of the numbers. But hold on, Seabiscuit! Before you trot off to the races and start rating guys, there are still a few more things you need to know. This is especially true if you were disappointed by your score.

One of the reasons that you haven't been dating well may be re-lated to a low overall score, or a dip in any one of your areas. If this is the case, you have work to do. You won't be ready to date until you can live with—or improve—your numbers, which means getting yourself into the best shape possible, both mentally and physically. You want to approach the dating world at your best, and with your highest score, so you won't be tempted to date down ever again.

The good news is that there are plenty of ways to increase your own score. In the next chapter I'll give you the tools to do exactly this, so that you will be ready to go out on a Friday night and feel proud about strutting your stuff.

4.

Bump Up Your Numbers

*Are you the best that you can be,
or is there someone fabulous hiding inside,
just waiting to jump out and be noticed?*

—REBA

THIS CHAPTER IS packed with great tips for getting your face and body numbers higher. But as you know, that's not all that counts. What's going on in your head is going to fuel your chances in any relationship. Read through the information on enhancing your personality and life situation numbers. There are lots of things you can do to increase your scores in these areas. And best of all, when you do, you'll feel much better about yourself.

If you are ready to change your rating, make sure you are making these improvements for the right reasons. If you want to change so that you can be the best person you can be, then you've got an excellent reason. However, if you want to be better just so that you can date up more effectively, then you're in for more disappointment.

Jessie

Jessie was trying to increase her score. The fresh-faced cashier at Stop & Shop hasn't been satisfied with the dates she's getting. After rating herself as a 5.25, she realized that she was dating out of her range. She wanted to increase her score, so she started hitting the gym more often than usual. In her mind a tight core will be her salvation, but Jessie didn't take into account how her numbers were already distributed. In fact, Jessie's body score was already high (8). Her face was in a comfortable range (6), but her personality (4) and life situation (3) scores were really pulling down her rating. Even if her grueling workouts managed to take her frame to the next level, her overall score would only increase to a 5.5! A better strategy would be to work on improving her life situation points. By raising that low score by 2 or 3 points, she could find herself in a whole different dating range!

SEE WHAT YOU'VE GOT

Take a look at your ratings in each category and see if the numbers are similar. If most of your scores are 6s and one area topped out at a 4, then you might want to work on that 4 first. Once your scores are even, or at least in the same range, then you can see if there is more room for improvement. Or, you might find that when you even out your score, you'll feel better about yourself overall, and rate yourself higher.

Another way to review the numbers is to look at your pre-average score. For example, if you scored a 25, which averages to a 6.25, but your goal is to be a 7, then you need to gain 3 points. You can add them in one category, or spread them over more than one area. For example, you can look over your face and body categories and see where you can pick up extra points. Then average your rating again and see if you've gotten to where you want to be.

Summer

Summer is a beautiful mature lady. She has a sales job and list of accomplishments under her well-coordinated belt. She has spent the many years since her divorce concentrating on her family, and her older children all agree that she's the best grandmother around. Now that all her children are finally out on their own, she's willing to get back into the dating world. She meets most of her dates through an online site and has recently been interested in one particular man, named Peter. After meeting him she decides that he is very good-looking, the right age, sweet as can be, and is doing some really neat things with his life. The only problem is that he rates slightly higher than her.

Summer has seen how her rating could have predicted the way that her past relationships went, and sees the same pattern again. However, she really likes Peter, and she's willing to do the work to get her ratings up to be equal to his. The last time she rated herself she scored a 6.5, which equals 26 overall points. If she can add just 2 more points her new total of 28 will equal a 7, which is what she rates Peter as.

Summer takes a quick look at the four areas of her life. Even though she's getting older, her face is still looking fresh. But she knows that she is at a higher weight than her doctor recommends. Her self-esteem has never been better, though her life situation can be considered as unconventional. She just moved in with her best friend so that they could share living expenses, and that situation is not likely to change anytime soon. Summer decides that the best place for her to get those two extra points is to slim down. She hopes to bring her body points from a 4 to a 6, and realizes with hard work, she might even beat her own expectations. All she needs is those two extra points to be in Peter's range and she knows it is a good health decision for her, too.

MORE ON SPIKES AND DIPS

When you look at your numbers, you will notice one of three things: your numbers are in the same range, you have one number that spikes high above the rest, or you have one number that takes a dip. None of these number patterns are better or worse: they are all just different. Consider yourself to have a dip or spike if one or two numbers are more than two or three points away from the rest.

Having a balanced set of numbers can mean a few different things. First, it can mean that you are at your peak in every area, or that you are not giving it your all in any area. When rating yourself, the biggest question is, "Am I happy with my overall score?" If you score a 6 and you are happy with a 6, then that's great. If you score a 6 and you are not happy with the number then you should take a closer look at the four areas and decide if you can increase your score so that you will be happy with yourself. Some things cannot change, and some things can. Concentrate on the things you can change.

Spikes are not much cause for concern. Having one number

jump up means you have a secret strength that you recognize is well above the rest of your attributes. But make sure to check your ego at the dating door. Having a secret strength can be both a blessing and a curse. The person whose number is considerably higher in face is always going to be tempted to judge themselves based on that one quality. If their face is an 8 they may think they deserve to date another 8, even if the rest of their score hovers around 5. That might lead to dating up, or worse, dating denial.

Another temptation a spiker can have is to believe that it is possible to bring the other scores up to the highest score. For example, if your face is an 8 but you are constantly trying to lose weight (that's got to sound familiar to someone!), you may hold off dating until you get the body to match that pretty face. But we all know that try as we might, it may never happen. So why are you wasting your time waiting? If you can truly raise your other numbers, then more power to you. But if you have been beating your head against a wall for years it might be time to let it go and thank God for that pretty face, or whatever spike you may have.

The best attitude for someone with a spike to have is to realize that their spike is a ringer. It lifts the low numbers and opens the dating doors to more possibilities. I promise, happiness will follow the woman who says, "I would be a 4 but I am blessed with a body that won't quit, so I'm a 6!" or "I'm a 7 because of my ability to parlay any business into a gold mine, but without this super IQ I'd probably be a 3!" Love your spike, but don't think your spike defines you. You are still the sum of all your qualities.

On the other hand, nothing spells depression like d-i-p. If you've rated yourself with a 7 for face, 7 for body, 8 for personality, and a 5 for life situation, then pull out the Kleenex, honey, 'cause you're going to need them. It's not that there is anything wrong with a 5 life situation—most people have 5s—but I know it's disappointing when you have such high scores in everything else. Getting a dipping score in any area will at first feel like a major setback.

Your dip can mean several different things. First, it can mean that you have one area in your life that you cannot change. As unfair as it seems, this does happen. I'm a big believer in self-improvement, because I know there is usually something you can do about either your face, body, personality, or life situation that will create a positive change. Read on through the end of the chapter to see what I mean. If you happen to have all high scores but one dip and you recognize that you can't bring the dip up, then count your many blessings and realize that you come by your overall 6 with flying colors.

A dip can also signal that you've been overcompensating in your other areas because you know you have a weakness. In my book that's called reality, and I applaud you for your hard work and success in beating your negative attributes. We all have them. However, if you are working your tail to the bone to keep your other numbers up to compensate for a dip you can't control then you could be feeling overworked and underpaid! Don't let resentment set in, and if you need to back off in other areas do it. These are your numbers so work 'em until they feel right.

If you have a dip because of a real setback, such as an illness or accident that has changed your body, or affected your employment, or if you have become a caretaker, try and hold on and roll with the flow. I'm sure you'll figure out a way to work with what you've got, or increase your other numbers to compensate for your current, and possibly fleeting, situation.

MAXIMIZING YOUR STRENGTHS

Lastly, you can increase your points by maximizing your strengths. If you scored higher in one area, think about increasing that area even more. For example, your happiness about your life situation can benefit your personality, and even your face and body. Just make sure that you don't fall into the trap of conceit, or you'll find yourself back in dating denial.

Now, let's take a look at each of the categories and see where there is room for a little improvement.

YOUR FACE

Do not be discouraged if you scored low on your face rating. We can bump that number up fairly easy. Many people think that heavily applied makeup or expensive plastic surgery are the only means available for changing the rating for your face. However, there are many makeover tricks you can follow today, in your own home, which will increase your face points without anesthesia or running up your credit card debt.

YOUR HAIR

An old proverb says, "There is safety in a multiple of counsel," and hair is no exception. Every girl needs at least one person that she can have an honest encounter with about her do. The best advice I get comes from one of my best friends from college, Atouzo. He studied business at school but quickly landed in fashion and hair design. He is brutally honest when I miss the mark with my hair, but excessively complimentary when I'm on point. Best of all, he's one of the most stylish people I know. He owns a swanky salon in downtown L.A. So if you don't have someone to give you the 411 on your hair, Atouzo has shared his best tips with you.

As he tells me, one of the fastest ways to transform your face is to change your hairstyle. A good haircut should frame and flatter your face, regardless of the current trends. Your hairdresser should take your lifestyle into account when cutting your hair. For example, if your job is very active, you shouldn't go for a hairstyle that will fall flat early in the day. Or, if you don't have lots of time to primp in the morning, then you will need a cut that is "wash and wear."

Atouzo's Tip #1: *You're going to spend money anyway, so you might as well spend it at the salon and look good.*

Keep your hair clean and well groomed at all times. Most hair stylists recommend a haircut every six to twelve weeks to cut off split ends and damaged hair. Covering up your gray is a personal decision, but I find that it definitely makes women look younger and more vibrant. Hair products have come a long way in the past few years. Discuss using them with your hair stylist, and see which options are right for your hair type.

Atouzo's Tip #2: *Just because they have scissors, honey, doesn't mean they should cut your hair.*

Do not skimp on a great haircut—it is always worth the price. A good haircut will last longer than a bad one, and will be more cost-effective over time. The perfect haircut is always done by a professional who can take both your hair type and your face shape into consideration. Bring in all the clippings you want, but a really good hairstylist will be able to match the latest trend and tailor it to your face, or tell you why it's the wrong haircut for your face or your hair type.

Hair types include three major categories: straight, wavy, or curly. Straight hair can range from fine blond hair to thick, coarse hair. Thin, straight hair often benefits from being colored, which adds texture and fullness to each strand. Simple, geometric haircuts, like bobs, are a natural for straight hair of any texture.

Atouzo's Tip #3: *All girls need to use product; we're not free like when we were in grade school.*

Wavy hair has lots of natural movement that can also be maximized with styling product, and can be blown straight or curly. Lightly layered hair is a natural choice for this hair type. Curly hair has great body, but may look dull or unruly. To maximize your hair's potential, choose a layered hairstyle (long or short) that cuts shape into curly hair. Hair product, including brilliantines, pomades, surface silkeners, and fixatives, can boost your hair's shine and calm down too much curl. For very coarse, curly hair, relaxing is a good choice, giving your hair a smoother and more manageable feel. Conditioners are also important for curly hair, which can have a tendency towards breakage and split ends.

Specific haircuts will look better on certain faces. There are seven basic facial shapes that are all easy to identify. Grab a soft tape measure and a free-standing mirror to see which type of face you have, and which type of haircut will look best for you.

> Atouzo's Tip #4: *I can't change your face, honey, don't complain about it; you just have to have the right hair around it.*

Oval. The oval face is 1.5 times longer than it is wide. If you have an oval face, your forehead will also be slightly wider than your jaw. Many haircuts and styles suit an oval face. However, the best styles are the ones that have layers at the height of your best features, such as your cheekbones, lips, or chin. Short layers at the top of the head can make your face look longer. However, if you have thick or curly hair, a blunt cut at any length can give you a "pyramid effect" instead of a softer, more rounded look.

Rectangular. Look for a narrow facial shape with both a square chin and hairline. The best haircuts for a rectangular face should add width to the sides of your head, such as a chin-length bob. Another way to create width is to add curls or waves to your hair. However, stay away from short layers, which will lend volume to the top, but further elongate the face. Either bangs or a side part will soften the squareness of this face. Extremely long or short hairstyles can make this face look longer.

Round. A round chin is the giveaway for this shape. The right hairstyle for this face will add height to the top of the head for a more oval look. You will want to cut the bulk away from the sides of your face as well. Stay away from a one-length haircut or blunt cuts on short hair. Instead, hairstyles that fall right below the chin and have wispy layers from the top down will soften and elongate the face.

Square. If you have a square jaw and hairline, you need a hairstyle that adds length and roundness to your face. Layered haircuts that frame the face around the jawline can soften your overall look. Your best options are short, spiky cuts or longer hairstyles with long layers starting at the jawline. Blunt-cut bangs or chin-length bobs will make your face look squarer.

Heart. This facial shape is widest at the temples and narrowest at the jawline, and is often accompanied by a pointed chin. Hairstyles for this shape need to add width at the jawline. A short hairstyle that keeps the top layers soft, or long, side-swept bangs are good options. Long, wavy layers can round off a pointed chin. Harsh, choppy layers or blunt cut bangs will not suit a heart-shaped face.

Pear. Look for a narrow forehead and wide jawline with a round chin. Your goal will be to add width to your forehead and temples, while drawing attention away from the roundness of your jaw. A chin-length haircut is best, and it should appear wide and full at the top. Curls are another good option to soften the face.

Diamond. A diamond shape is widest at the cheekbones but narrow at the forehead and chin. You will want to add width to the forehead and soften the cheekbones to give an illusion of an oval face. A low side part and a sweep of hair brushed across the forehead adds width to the face. Asymmetric haircuts are another good option, especially for curly or wavy styles.

YOUR TEETH

Healthy teeth and a healthy smile are always beautiful things. Your teeth are not only a huge part of your face; your smile is what people are looking at when you make a first impression. Those little white pearls are showing themselves as you convey your personality and life situation.

There are some easy and inexpensive ways to improve the overall look and health of your teeth. Right now, teeth whitening is all the rage. The quick effects of teeth whitening can be amazing and sometimes all you'll need to go from an okay smile to a brilliant one. I've found that the cheaper products on the market work just as well as the more expensive options, but may be a little more cumbersome. I've gotten great results by following these easy steps:

1. Get a sports mouth guard from your local sporting goods store. They soften and adhere to your teeth after you boil them.

2. Put the teeth whitener into the mouth guard and bite down. Or use the whitening strips directly on your teeth, and then use the mouth guard on top. Lock in the whitener and hit the sack. When you wake up, you'll have pearly whites.

A consultation with a dentist or orthodontist may be necessary if you have more significant problems with your teeth. Don't be afraid of the pain or the cost; there are many options available at all price ranges. These range from invisible braces that last just a year, to a retainer appliance that can change your bite and the overall shape of your face. Anything you do to improve your oral health, be it breath fresheners, teeth whitening, or orthodontics, will increase your face points. Imagine, you could have Julia Roberts's smile in just a few weeks!

YOUR SKIN

The secret to beautiful skin is to keep it as clean and supple as possible. Good skin is a sign of youthfulness and will make you more attractive. Your daily routine should consist of a cleanser, toner, and moisturizer (always with a built-in SPF of at least 15). Find a company that is compatible to your skin type and use a line of products that are complementary to each other. My mom tells me, "Moisturize all over every day, 'cause you never know where you'll age!"

Staying out of the sun is the best way to limit your exposure to its harmful rays. Excessive tanning not only damages your skin, it will cause you to wrinkle prematurely. If you have to be in the sun, protect your face by applying sunscreen and use a bronzer.

If you have frequent breakouts, you might want to think about prescription medications that can really help with blemishes. Many birth control pills tout acne relief; check with your gynecologist. Some people suffer from oily skin, which is not attractive. There are plenty of products on the market to help. An oil-absorbing pad that you can dab on your face throughout the day would help. If you're using too many drying agents your skin may overcompensate and produce too much oil.

Please also consider changing your makeup. If you haven't had a professional department store consultation in more than two years, consider replenishing your products for a new look. In general, I find that men prefer less makeup than more. The more natural trend in makeup supports my findings. That heavily made-up face is really a thing of the past, and can make you look more like a dinosaur than a daisy.

Perhaps the best advice for glowing skin is to get plenty of sleep and eat properly. A lack of sleep really shows on your face with dark circles under the eyes and a sallow, drawn complexion. Seven to eight hours a night is the minimum requirement for healthy sleep. Fish oil supplementation and foods high in omega-3 fatty acids, like salmon, are also great for your skin. By increasing your fish consumption to as little as three times a week, you'll see the difference in the texture and tone of your face quickly.

YOUR ATTITUDE

You would be surprised by how much your attitude affects your facial ratings. If you are smiling and attentive you will be perceived by others as more attractive. You don't have to be Miss Congeniality all the time, but you can allow your face to rest in a pleasant expression. A furrowed brow or a blank stare is not going to make you attractive to others.

Be conscious of how your inward attitude may be affecting your looks. Take a quick picture of yourself today for a reality check of how you look. Continue taking pictures with different expressions until you find one you like. Then remember that expression, and try to do it whenever you want to feel good about your face. Chances are, that's when you will look your best.

YOUR BODY

If you are less than pleased with your body rating, you are not alone. Most of us are on an uphill battle with our bodies. Our bodies naturally age and deteriorate, but the human condition is to want them to appear athletic and youthful. While almost none of us can have a perfect 10 body, we can all bump up our numbers by at least a digit or two.

I know that just thinking about getting into better shape sends many women into a tailspin. Some are so afraid to try that they completely give up before they even step foot in a gym. Others do drastic and crazy things to get results, although they are usually only good in the short term. My first suggestion is to prioritize your body in terms of health first, and sex appeal second. Once you incorporate different strategies to feel better, you'll have an easier time working out and will get better results.

If you are trying to increase your body rating, increase your activity and additional points will follow. That's because a better body is a healthier body. Doing something active every day is a good goal that most can achieve. Find an athletic activity that works your muscles and your heart. Don't let a day go by without getting your blood pumping and muscles moving for at least thirty minutes. You can take a walk or run in the morning or hit the gym at night, or consider fun activities like biking, tennis, dancing, yoga, or karate.

My three best dieting tips are so simple, anyone can follow them. First, dump your vice. If sugar is your fancy, get rid of it. If you have a yearning for salty snacks, stay away from them. If beer or pizza is what you crave, don't have it. It may not be easy but it's probably the one thing that is keeping you from getting that body you want.

The second tip is even easier. Eat more. That's right, I want you to eat more foods that are good for you. After you dump your big vice you can add in more of those healthy foods, like fruits, veggies, whole grains, low-fat proteins like chicken and fish, and lots and lots of water.

The third tip is not so much a task, but a reminder. Remember that a lot of people overeat because of stress or for comfort. You may be eating because it's easier than thinking or dealing with the life you have. But when you dump your vice you will have to deal with reality. Dealing with life can be hard, but it will be a heck of a lot easier when you have a better body score. So dump your vice, eat more healthy foods, and sort out your problems. If you can do these three things, I guarantee that you will increase your body score.

YOUR POSTURE

Do you look better lying down than standing up? Do you feel uncomfortable when you are walking for long periods of time? Do your clothes look better before you put them on? If you answered yes to any of these questions, then you may need to change your posture. The way you stand is key to the appearance of your body. By improving your posture, you can change the way you present yourself to others almost immediately.

Different body types are going to be prone to different postures. Likewise, different body types look better or worse with different postures. Some tall girls tend to hunch over to try and make themselves seem shorter. But if you do this, you'll end up being a tall girl who looks slouchy. Many slim girls tend to hold their arms wider or more spread out in order to appear bigger. It makes them look robotic and certainly less suave or charming. Heavyset women tend to hide behind their crossed arms, which also doesn't work, especially as you get older and your arms get flabby.

To improve your posture, try to keep your head consistently level with your eyes facing forward. This will redirect your whole body toward positive posture. Stand tall and practice walking with a book on your head, don't let it drop! Your gait should be as long as possible. Your strides should be propelled by your hips, with your arms casually falling to the side.

Your shoulders are the second factor in good posture. Your shoulders need to form right angles to the neck: they should not be curled in or slouched down. A slight arch in the back will bring your chest and backside out. Taking this position when you sit or stand not only improves your posture, but it will support your lower back.

YOUR CLOTHES

Another simple way to raise your body rating is with your wardrobe. If your hair is the frame for the face, then clothes are the frame for the body. You can accent your positive body features and de-emphasize your negative ones with clothing. The trick is to only wear clothes that make you look good and feel great. Go through your closet and throw out everything that makes you feel less than stunning.

Every girl has a "trouble" area, or at least some part of her body she doesn't like. The information below will help you identify your body type and address your "trouble areas" to look your best! One trick I've learned is that black is a wardrobe assistant's best friend. If you have a body area that you find too prominent, then acquire at least four items to cover it in black (four shirts or four pairs of pants, for example). Basic black works for all the seasons, in all climates, day and night. You can never have too much black in your closet.

There are other tricks of the trade that I've learned over the years. First, if your legs are short, wear higher heels, all the time. This doesn't mean to the gym, but give yourself a little lift everywhere else you go. If you're thick in the middle, wear a more tailored jacket. This seems to be counterintuitive, but it works. The goal is to create length by creating curves, even if you don't really have them.

There are four basic body types. The *inverted triangle* is heavier on top than on bottom, with a generous bust, full back, and wide middle with narrow hips and slender legs. Some call this the *round* or *apple shape*. You would look best wearing tops with narrow collars to avoid drawing attention to your full bust. Tops with V necks or scoop necks will elongate and slenderize your neck. Pencil skirts that show off your slender legs, or hip-hugging jeans to accentuate your curves offer a range of choices for day and evening.

In contrast, a *pear-shaped body* is generally bottom-heavy. This body type has a slender neck, narrow shoulders, smaller bust, as well as a shapely waist, generous lower hips, and full thighs. Choose hugging tops to help bring attention to your slender upper body, and bottoms made of flowing fabrics.

A *rectangular body* refers to when your upper and lower torso are equal in size, with an average bust, undefined waist, flat bottom, and slender legs. This body type should avoid turtlenecks and tops with necklines above your collarbone. Instead, you can elongate your torso with tunics. Avoid skirts with gathered waists as they can make your waist look thick. Instead, choose skirts with dropped waists to slenderize your look.

Lastly, an *hourglass body* has a small bone structure, defined waist, curved hips, protruding bottom, and shapely legs. Make sure you accentuate your curves well. Avoid baggy clothes, and flaunt your defined waist with belts. Choose tops that sit at your waist, and pants that are flattering to your stomach and rear end.

No matter what your body type is, I've found that we can all use a little help that usually starts with our foundation. That's right, I'm talking about your bra. Most women are wearing the wrong size bra, or one that doesn't suit their shape. Some women even think of plastic surgery before they look into buying new bras! All it takes is a couple of hours with a real expert who can fit you perfectly. Find a legitimate lingerie shop or a department store for the best advice. You'll also find that your clothes fit better, and your bra is more comfortable when you are properly sized.

YOUR PERSONALITY

Changing your personality rating is going to be the hardest of the four areas. Without getting into the whole nature versus nurture debate, let's assume that your personality comes from both your genetics and your lifestyle. Most of us have never thought to change our personality, but that might be what is holding you back from dating the way you want.

Many people believe that their personality is who they really are. People lose limbs, jobs, hair, and that youthful glow, but underneath it all their personality remains. I like to think of this in a different way; that your personality is the way you represent your soul and your spirit. Because of this, I believe that every person can redefine the way they represent themselves. Though it is tempting to use your past hurts as a justification for your personality, you do not have to wear your wrongs like a badge. It is possible to change, and to become a better person. You can show the world, and especially the person you want to date, who you really are.

Personality Inventory

If you are trying to raise your points in this area the first thing you should do is take inventory of who you are right now. Circle the qualities from this list that you already possess:

Open	*Stubborn*	*Mean*	*Patient*
Giving	*Aggressive*	*Passive*	*Nervous*

Tenacious	*Obstinate*	*Soothing*	*Cheery*
Sharing	*Pushy*	*Loud*	*Dry*
Odd	*Hilarious*	*Droll*	*Unusual*
Peculiar	*Curious*	*Willful*	*Dogged*
Uplifting	*Promising*	*Depressing*	*Elegant*
Straight	*Shifty*	*Shy*	*Opportunist*
Polished	*Poised*	*Charming*	*Loving*
Awkward	*Inept*	*Difficult*	*Self-conscious*
Smiling	*Shocking*	*Slow*	*Snooty*
Kind	*Consoling*	*Calming*	*Reassuring*
Forgiving	*Rude*	*Unpredictable*	*Victim*
Flexible	*Flaky*	*Questionable*	*Fake*
Amusing	*Quaint*	*Witty*	*Weird*
Spoiled	*Needy*	*Anal*	*Touchy*
Graceful	*Phony*	*Truthful*	*Elitist*
Honest	*Frank*	*Candid*	*Reliable*
Serious	*Comical*	*Strange*	*Boring*
Lofty	*Quick*	*Bright*	*Funny*
Easygoing	*Tight*	*Professional*	*Lazy*
Comforting	*Nurturing*	*Helpful*	*Greedy*
Generous	*Accurate*	*Benevolent*	*Exact*

Next, take a look at the traits you circled and put an X through the ones you do not like. Then look at the traits you did not circle, and underline the ones you wish you had. This quick inventory will show you why you are not giving yourself more personality points. You may not even realize that you are reflecting traits that you do not like. Knowing this should help you get rid of those negative traits.

I know that this concept isn't rocket science, but it will take hard work. Just acknowledging that you want to get rid of a personality trait is the first step. Understanding what you really want to reflect to the rest of the world is the second step. If you put an X through a trait then try to find the opposite of that trait and put a dark circle around it. Similarly if you underlined a trait that you want to have, then find the opposite of that trait and put a dark X on it. Stay away from personifying the Xs and try your hardest to reflect the ones you circled. Change will not happen overnight, but you can begin to reflect more of the inner person you want to be, which is how you will increase your personality points.

THERAPY

Getting to the root of what is keeping you from living the life you aspire to might require professional help. A trained and licensed therapist might be able to point out the areas of your life that need further examination. You may have some past hurt or mistaken understanding that is keeping you from expressing yourself in a way that represents the real you. Other life events, such as abuse, neglect, violence, abandonment, or loss, can cause us to hide or overcompensate our feelings. You may need to walk through some difficult emotions before you can get to a place where you can be yourself again.

Therapy is especially helpful if you want to raise your personality points and have tried on your own but to no avail. Sometimes it takes someone on the outside to provide a fresh perspective. There are probably things in your life that have a direct connection to your personality that you have never put together. As you reveal more about yourself to a counselor, they will be able to see the link. Sometimes, just realizing why you act a certain way can give you the power to change.

TWELVE-STEP GROUPS

If you are already aware of your shortcomings, especially if you are struggling with addictions, a twelve-step group can help you. Many people who go to therapy are also involved with twelve-step programs. This popular format provides a way to manage uncontrollable behaviors and thoughts. When you get control of your thoughts and behaviors you are going to be more capable of reflecting your inner person. This will in turn ramp up your personality rating.

You do not have to be an alcoholic to go to a twelve-step program. There are many twelve-step groups for other vices, including sexaholics, workaholics, codependents, overeaters, undereaters, and even clutteraholics. Look online to find a group that meets near you, or offers an online group. There is no obligation other than just trying to be a better person.

DEVELOPING A SPIRITUAL SIDE

If your personality is a reflection of who you are, then you should be able to communicate what you believe. Take some time to find God. As you develop a real relationship with God and your religious community, your personality will reflect your spirit. If you allow yourself to get completely caught up in your physical self you will seem shallow to others. But if you allow your spirit to exist with your other attributes, you will become a deeper, more balanced person.

Religion provides you with a bigger picture in which to frame your life. If you only think about yourself and your current needs you will narrow your personality rating. But if you can see the more eternal perspective, which is a more loving perspective, and a perspective that links us all together, then your personality will bloom.

Even if you have no interest in hitting a pew or singing with the choir you can still find God and a deeper spirituality. Think of your spirit as the being inside of you that you can't explain with brain synapses and scientific reflexes. You can learn more about this side of yourself in so many different ways. You can discover your spirituality with a simple prayer, by talking to another family member, or search through your bookcase and read up. Sometimes something as simple as watching the sunset or holding a baby can reconnect you with that spiritual girl inside.

YOUR LIFE SITUATION

You might guess that in our image-obsessed world we would judge ourselves most sternly in the body and face categories. However, I find that there is often another area where we judge ourselves critically and that gets the most attention. Your life situation rating is the hardest to define, the hardest to change, and certainly the hardest to improve.

If your personality is the expression of your inner self, then your life situation is the vehicle for this expression. Your life situation reflects your true desires and supports the growth of who you are inside. It contains the terms that govern your life: where you live, where you work, and who you choose to surround yourself with. It can provide a framework for your social life or dominate your hierarchy of needs. It can offer opportunities or it can hold you back from being who you know you could be.

For example, if you believe family is important, then surround yourself with those that love you. If you feel that life is all about having fun, then fill your garage full of gear and go for it. If your work ethic is what defines your happiness, then hop on the corporate ladder or set out your own shingle and start a business.

These are the parts of your life situation that are easy to define. However, we all know that life isn't always fair. Some people fall into luxury and comfort while others work for years to eke out a meager living. There are parts of your life situation that you can manage, and other parts where you have no control. And there are countless variables that can change a life situation in a heartbeat, such as a handicap, a major award, or a pregnancy.

There are millions of ways to make our lives great even when bad things happen, especially if we never saw them coming. For example, losing your job can be a devastating blow. Initially you will need to take a couple of steps back, so take advantage of that time and get ready to make a big change. You might want to go back to school. Maybe you could live off student loans long enough to be the professional you've dreamed of. Or you might decide to make a more lateral career change.

Sometimes you just have to sit back and ride a bad life situation out. If you have been a victim of a natural disaster, diagnosed with a disease, or are going through a divorce, you may have to just hang in there for now. Sometimes doing nothing at all is the hardest part. Try to find joy in simple things, like starting a puzzle or picking up a guitar. Rent every Hitchcock movie you can get your hands on or just look through old picture albums. Being still is a good time to find pleasure in simple things.

DEALING WITH LIFE'S INEVITABILITIES

There are also aspects of life that require planning. One such situation is dealing with our aging parents. Being a caretaker is a weighty experience but if we learned one thing from Disney's *The Lion King*, there really is a circle of life. I believe that everyone has an obligation to the happiness of their family members. But while you may be responsible for taking care of your aging parents, you are not obligated to stop living. If you are not in this life situation yet, it's time to start planning for it. And if you are, here are a couple of good tips I've been given.

First, try letting your parents live vicariously through you. Go to dinner with friends, go shopping, experience life, and then come home and share your stories. Also ask for their help, and get them to become a more active participant in your life. Not only will they be doing you a favor, you are helping them feel needed, building their self-esteem.

EFFECTING CHANGE IN YOUR LIFE SITUATION

Start your life situation change with a piece of paper and a phone. Write down one category of your life where you would like to see change: your job, your home, or your free time.

Next, write down one thing that you absolutely love. This can be as simple as "coffee," "organic food," or "Israeli dancing." Then write down everything you can think of that has to do with that item. If you wrote down organic food then you might follow with a few of your favorite organic markets, free-range chicken, organic strawberries, or organic pesticide vendors.

Then consider how this interest relates to the category you

chose. If you want a new career, next list your expertise: do you have accounting skills, a class C driver's license, management skills, or sales ability? Ask yourself where your skill fits in to your favorite things list and then make a call. Call the market or the free-range farm and ask questions. Ask them if they have a need for someone with your skills. Ask them who they work with, what vendors sell to them, or who they sell to or service. Try to fill up the paper with leads and potential jobs.

If you are looking for a change in your home, see how this same thing can be better integrated into your home life. If you wrote organic food, see if you are living within the parameters of an organic life. What can you change about your home or home life to better integrate yourself with this word? Do you live in or near a toxic environment (speaking either metaphorically or literally), or can you happily thrive right where you are?

Or think about how you currently spend your free time, and see how it relates to your list. Do you use your spare time in a way that is in keeping with an organic lifestyle? Research how you can get more involved in this community. Can you join a CSA, community supported agricultural group, or organic food co-op? Would you like to volunteer in some way or help create the next organic product? The point is to integrate what you love into your life. By doing so, you can make a positive change in your life situation.

FINDING BALANCE

Whatever an improved life situation looks like for you, it must have balance. Whether you are trying for a moderate or 14k-gold lifestyle you are going to lose points if it is lacking basic elements or is too heavy in certain areas. For example, if you have a great-paying job but it requires that you work all the time, are you better off than your friends who work less but earn less? The decision is for you to make, but I can tell you from experience, the best life situations are the ones that contain lots of hard work and lots of time for play.

Take an honest look at your life in each of these areas to see how far or close you are to your ultimate goals. Find the areas that you can change with the least amount of effort, and work on changing those first. Then find the area where you can make the biggest impact on your life and work on making improvements to it. There are no right or wrong answers for each of these areas: their significance in your life is as individual as you are. Only you will know when you have achieved the right balance.

- Activity
- Entertainment
- Family
- Friends
- Hobbies
- Home
- Location
- Religion
- Roommates
- Transportation
- Work

I lived through many life situations in a very short time. I got married my first year of college, quit school, gave birth to my daughter, and then found myself getting divorced. My personal dramas had me living a middle-aged life by the time I was twenty-two, and believe me, I wasn't happy. I knew that in order for me to find peace, my life situation had to change, and fast. I don't take full credit for all the changes, but I made some choices that gave me the advantages I needed in order to improve my life situation.

First I went back to school and lived in campus family housing. I had an instant support network with all the families around me. Then I made some untraditional choices with a bit of ingenuity, and made the best of a hard situation. I doubled up with my baby in one bedroom and had another student move in with us in my second room for free in exchange for some light nanny duties. My grants and loans paid the bills, and I joined a baby-sitting exchange with other women who were in the same set of circumstances. This gave me some free time and plenty of access to the social activities on campus. This exchange program turned out to be one of my biggest reliefs. By taking advantage of the service, I was also able to start work during school with an internship at a local radio station. I found a career that I was passionate about, and have been working in this industry to this day. I can definitely say that I improved my life situation from my worst score of 4 to now, when my best score is 7.

YOUR RATING WILL CHANGE EVERY DAY, AND THAT'S OKAY
There are times when you'll be feeling better, or worse, about your body or your face. Some days you will walk out of your office with a smile on your face, and some days you will hate your job.

Then there are the unplanned events of life that can dramatically affect your score. A change to your personal health is a good example. Because these events are unforeseen, it's important to make your other numbers as high as they can be. For example, Jesse Billauer has overcome huge adversity, but still has a great rating.

A former professional surfer, Jesse's rich dark hair and eyes to match are many a girl's dream, and his friendly, down-to-earth personality makes him just a joy to be around. This Santa Monica surfer founded the Life Rolls On Foundation, which raises money for victims of spinal cord injuries. Jesse hosts frequent galas and parties with celebs like Paris Hilton and Kelly Slater.

It would be no surprise that Jesse has a hot girlfriend who is totally into him, except for the fact that Jesse is confined to a wheelchair. His pro surfing career ended when he was surfing at Zuma Beach, California, back in 1996 and was pushed headfirst into a shallow sandbar. Jesse fractured his neck and severed his spinal cord, leaving him a quadriplegic. However, his numbers still work in his favor. Jesse has an amazing face, fantastic personality, and incredible life situation. Even though his body points are very low, he has managed to maximize his assets.

By taking the time to maximize your assets, and correct the parts of your score that you were unhappy with, you will be able to face the dating world with power, and personal conviction, just like Jesse. The rest of the book will teach you more about how to perceive and judge others. For now, I hope that you have learned that there are better ways for you to perceive and judge yourself, to become the best person you can be. This is important not just for dating others, but for loving yourself.

5.

Let's Get Rating

IT'S TIME TO start rating potential dates. You will be able to instantly assess the same four categories that you have been thinking about for yourself: face, body, personality, and life situation. But now you'll turn the tables, and rate any man you are interested in, or who is interested in you.

IT'S ALL ABOUT THE SUM OF THE PARTS

The problem with the way people traditionally rate others, especially in the dating world, is that they tend to only rate on one or two attributes. I remember a local TV show back in the nineties called *Tens*. The show usually took place on a beach and was hosted by a bikini-clad duo who scoured the area looking for what they considered the perfect 10 body. I can't remember how the rest of the show went, but I was definitely turned off by how shallow it seemed to judge people based solely on how they looked wearing a tiny piece or two of Lycra on Daytona Beach. Don't get me wrong: I'm not discounting how great it would be to have killer abs and buns of steel. But I also know that there's more to life, and certainly more ways to judge another person besides a lucky set of genes and their workout habits.

The goal of the Rating Game is to not get caught up on any single attribute a guy has, like their smile, or their red car, or their beach house, and disregard the rest of them. There are going to be plenty of men who have one attribute or another that you find attractive. However, you are looking to create synchronicity with a whole person. Instead, you are going to be taking everything about each guy into account in a very short time. If your numbers match, you will have a better chance of entering into a relationship that might actually work. Remember, you are not looking for someone that scores a perfect 10, you are looking for someone who is perfect for you.

Your range is someone who rates the same whole number as you. There can be varying degrees in the fractional points. When you find someone in your range, you'll feel secure and comfortable right from the start. If you rate them higher than yourself, you may feel like you have to try hard just to keep them. You may get insecure, jealous, or possessive. If you rate higher than him the tables turn; he might try to hold you back or suppress you in some way so that he feels like you are on the same level.

GUESS WHO'S BETTER THAN HIM?
If you think you can land a 10, think again. These are the absolute 10s in each category:

Face

- McDreamy
- McSteamy
- Your trainer at the gym

Body

- Abercrombie & Fitch models
- Water polo players
- Mark Wahlberg modeling Calvin Klein, circa 1992

Personality

- Ryan Seacrest
- Penelope Cruz's boyfriends
- Barack Obama

Life Situation

- Seal
- The Donald
- Harry and William, Princes of Wales

Tiffany

My friend Tiffany thought she had it all. I met her right after she moved to L.A. from New York City. I was so impressed by her New York class and her Chanel coats. This twenty-seven-year-old "party girl" had worked at a top clothing designer's corporate office, and had the designer outfits to match. Tiffany went to a very prestigious East Coast university, and she had beauty to go with her high GPA. So it was no wonder that Tif was perfectly pleased when she met a well-known L.A. socialite while getting a mani-pedi at her favorite salon in West Hollywood. Brad was well groomed but not handsome at forty-five years old. He had a personality as big as his smile and charm to boot. The two chatted over complimentary cocktails, and had exchanged phone numbers before Tiffany's nails were even dry.

Having come from a wealthy family, Tiffany was not overly impressed with Brad's money. She did, however, take notice of Brad's choice lifestyle. Brad is welcomed at all the A-list events and is known by everybody who is anybody in Hollywood. The two enjoyed each other's company, and, despite the age difference, seemed to be well suited.

One night Brad decided to express his fondness for Tiffany physically. He gave her extra time and attention at dinner. As the evening progressed he ushered her out onto the patio of his home set atop the coveted Hollywood Hills. She breathed in the night air and took in the skyline view of the city. When Brad made his move, he was shocked to find that Tiffany was completely unresponsive. The next day, Tiffany's number was deleted from his cell phone, and she never heard from him again.

Tiffany liked Brad, yet she wasn't physically attracted to him. While they were dating, she chose to focus on the qualities she did appreciate, namely, his social calendar. In Tiffany's eyes, Brad's lifestyle and personality were incredible, but she couldn't get past his less-than-appealing looks. This doesn't make her shallow, it makes her human. Brad would have never uttered a word to Tiffany had she not been so beautiful.

Tif and I ran the numbers and found that she perceived Brad

as a 7, but she thought that she was a hot 9. The numbers spoke for themselves: Brad was not an equal match for her. She would always be disappointed with him, and he was smart enough to know it after the first polite rejection.

Tiffany's story illustrates how one or two impressive qualities can tempt us to enter a relationship with the wrong person. In your world, think about the know-it-all in high school who was the teacher's pet, but couldn't find anyone to hang out with him at recess. Academically he was a 10, and even though he might have become a dot-com zillionaire, unless he learned some social skills his braininess still won't take him very far in the dating scene. Even the good-looking football player or cheerleader will be in for a rough life if they decide to date solely based on their looks.

SCORE SOME MEN

All attributes are created equal, but few men (or women) can really tout the total package. Most have varying degrees of fineness. Some have a better body and a less thrilling life situation, or a fabulous personality and just a pretty face. This is why it is the overall score that is important. So don't assume that some guy with a 9 body is an overall 9, or someone with a 4 life situation can't have an 8 personality. The law of averages lets us know you must add up all the attributes and divide them by four.

The numbers are defined in the same way as when we rate ourselves. When you meet someone, give them the benefit of the doubt, and start your mind with a clean slate and a score of 5. Then, work your way up or down the scale from there. Here's what the numbers represent for the men out there:

10 = PERFECTION

10s are given in any category only when there is no room for improvement. The perfect model's face. The body of Michelangelo's prized *David*. A veritable Superman fighting for truth, beauty, and the American way of life, while at the same time helping little old ladies cross the street. A life situation that includes an unending supply of cash, great taste in restaurants, and no baggage that would make Dr. Phil wince.

While you'll definitely meet men who rate a 10 in any given area, a person who has 10s in all four categories is as rare as the Great Star of Africa diamond. Bestow 10s when they're deserved but keep in mind that giving out a 10 is like putting someone on a pedestal—they're likely to fall off. And remember, it only takes one 9 to bring down a perfect score.

9 = THE BEST IN THE ROOM

A 9 in any area indicates that a man has made the most with the hand life has dealt him. It's not just a pretty face; it's maximizing it with styled hair and a great smile. It's not only that they look hot in clothes; it's a toned body underneath. Wealth and success can make any man attractive, but what are they doing with it? A personality that lights up the room is wonderful, but a 9 has strived to understand himself to become more. Most 9s have worked their butts off to get that number, so hand it out as you would a trophy or a blue ribbon.

8 = GREAT

I know that there were kids out there who were just naturally smart and didn't have to study or work hard, while the rest of us spent every waking hour studying to get that A. It's the same thing with an 8: this man may be blessed with a beautiful face, can crawl into a freezer at Cold Stone and eat his way out without gaining an ounce, has the Midas touch when it comes to life, or knows exactly what to say and how to act in any situation. You are not allowed to deduct points because it looks too easy for them: you have no idea (yet) how hard they have worked to get here.

7 = GOOD

This rating should be absolutely satisfying. It's well above average and its qualities are all positive, as 7 is the lowest of the best numbers. It's the smallest house in the best neighborhood. A flawless diamond but small in carat weight. A man who deserves a good steak, but can't afford filet mignon. A 7 has a very good-looking face or a nice body. Natural 7s could be 8s if they tried; there's room for improvement but many men are content with living a 7 life—and there's nothing wrong with that.

6 = ABOVE AVERAGE

Think of 6 as "comfortable." A 6 face is welcoming but isn't really great-looking. A 6 body is inviting but won't win a Mr. Universe pageant by a long shot. Personalities are likely to be warm and caring, but also flawed. The same holds true for life situation.

Caution! I've known many a friend that has used the *P* word when they meet a 6, as in "He has so much potential . . ." But you can never count on change. In reality, there's nothing wrong with being a 6, which is why most guys who are 6s are happy to stay that way.

5 = AVERAGE

The majority of us are 5s. That's why it's called "average." Go to any shopping mall and people-watch; you'll see dozens of the average American 5. These 5s are generally nice-looking, pleasing, and personable, but can be wonderfully flawed. The average American man's body is less than svelte, standing at 5'9" tall and weighing in at 180 pounds. They live in cities, towns, suburbs, and even farms, but never in a penthouse. They're the neighbor next door who will help you out in a pinch, but will occasionally drive you nuts with his loud music (and it's always a band you hate). The best thing about 5s is that there are so many of them. The dating field for 5s is highly populated. And if you're happy with a 5, feel good knowing that so are the majority of women out there.

4 = OKAY

4 is a gray area somewhere between average and "Houston, we have a problem." Doling out 4s is serious business. If you start out with "average," are you going to drop a point for a facial feature you don't care for? A 4 is like a nice house with a big mortgage—maybe you wouldn't mind living there, but you wouldn't want to pay the bills.

3 = BELOW AVERAGE

When you spot a 3, it can seem like the train has arrived at the station and you are now in Problemsville. The quirks, traits, and nuances that can apply to 4s and 5s are now getting more serious, and are not so easily overlooked or tolerated. If your friends are asking, "What do you see in him?" chances are he's a 3 in at least one area.

A 3 has to work twice as hard on a problem as a 4 would—and that's *if* the person wants to resolve that issue. No doubt about it, a 3 is a negative number with no warm fuzzies attached. Be careful when giving out this score because it will be hard to average in with the rest of the numbers. However, if it is deserved, then take a minute to digest exactly what you are really seeing.

2 = NOT GOOD

On the evolutionary scale, a 2 is like the lizard that has barely crawled out of the pond. A 2 in any category is screaming, "Unacceptable!" The opposite of a 2 on this scale is a 9, and as much as a 9 is well deserved, so is a 2. Yes, there are times when people hit this number because of circumstances: a bankruptcy can decimate a life situation; an accident or illness can lower a body score. But those are exceptions. Typically, the trait or condition that warrants a 2 will have you wishing the lizard would turn around and slither back into the pond.

1 = CALL SECURITY

One word: run! This is the lowest of the lows. If a 10 is absolute perfection, then a 1 is the slime at the bottom of the barrel. Actually, the chance that you'll actually meet someone with a 1 rating is rare. A 1 rating reflects the ultimate in what you *don't* want, need, or value. A 1 rating is so bad that you're not likely to be interested enough in the guy to even bother rating him. More than likely, if you do hand over a 1, it will be when you're rerating him after you've found out something that is devastating and totally unacceptable. At that time, you're at the "don't let the door hit you on the way out" part of the relationship anyway.

Lisa

Lisa, an ambitious 8, giggled nervously as she recalled her last relationship. "Gary was sweet but I could never understand why he wouldn't do more with himself," she said with a little guilt in her voice. Lisa lives in a high-rise apartment in the best part of town. She drives a luxury car, has a great job, a beautiful face, and a toned body. When she met Gary, she was impressed. He was very good-looking and Lisa thought that if he lost some weight they would look like a couple out of a magazine. "I was always on him about what he was eating, about wearing nicer clothes, and getting a new car. I thought if he looked better, he'd feel better about himself." Her critiquing extended to his career choice as well. "It would never enter his mind to apply for a promotion," she told me in an exasperated tone.

It was no surprise to me when their relationship cooled. But it wasn't Lisa who did the cooling. Gary called it quits because he was tired of the constant nagging. Afterward, when Lisa rated Gary, she realized that "he was a 6 and he was comfortable being a 6. My agenda didn't stand a chance." Now she realizes that she must have made him miserable, trying to change him into something he wasn't.

THE CATEGORIES

The categories for judging others are the same ones we used for judging yourself. The first two categories are immediate and visual, and while it may sound superficial, let's get real; it's the face and bod that attracts us in the first place. How many of us would really cross a room to talk to someone who wasn't attractive, on the chance that his personality or life situation would be stunning?

A MAN'S FACE

The face is a fascinating area to evaluate because it is the one thing that most people feel they have little control over. This is not entirely true. While we can't control the proportions of our face, and most men aren't interested in enhancing their faces with makeup, we can determine how others project positive or negative feelings through their facial gestures. I think that the face, especially for men, is actually an appendage of their personality, and a closer look can help us rate more accurately.

We use our faces to communicate in ways that we may not even be conscious of, and the residue this communication leaves behind can offer up some important clues. You can tell a lot about what is going on inside a person by their face, even if they are wearing a poker face. Look for a furrowed brow, or deep creases on the forehead. These can signal a worrier, or someone who is unhappy with themselves. On the other hand, laugh lines around the eyes or a quirky grin can signal someone who is fun to be with and who doesn't take himself too seriously.

Then notice how his face changes during conversation. Can you clearly see expressions that reflect the words "happy and confident"? Does his face invite you to talk? Or is it sad, bored, lonely, or depressed? Does it make you want to keep walking? Does he give off an air of superiority, making him seem unapproachable?

How is the eye contact? When you are talking with someone, you are supposed to maintain eye contact. That shows the other person that you are listening and engaged. If he is looking past you during a conversation, particularly if he is looking at other women, or if his head and eyes are cast downwards, it will make communication difficult. Looking down and not maintaining eye contact shows insecurity.

Rating someone else's face is generally easy. Although there are considerations that need to be taken into account, basically, you know what attracts you. Then, look closer for the physical details:

Hair. Does his haircut accentuate his face? Is the style up-to-date? Is it clean? Is it touchable? If he shaves his head, is it clean-shaven?

Facial hair. While his eyebrows don't have to be waxed, there should be two of them—no monobrows! Is he clean-shaven? If he has a beard or mustache, are they trimmed and well shaped? Do they complement his face? If he wears sideburns, are they even and trimmed? Is nose and ear hair trimmed?

Eyes. Are the eyes clear, bright, and awake? Or are they tired and sleepy? Do they look healthy? Are the whites of the eyes white? Is eye contact inviting?

Teeth. Is there a nice smile? Are the teeth clean, straight, and cared for?

Skin. Does it have a healthy color? Is it well taken care of? Are there oily patches? Is the skin dry or chapped? Is it blemished, scarred? Are there wrinkles?

A MAN'S BODY

Judging a man's physique is one of the easiest things to do. Though people come in different shapes and sizes, it is easy to judge whether a person is taking care of their body or neglecting it. A quick glance at the body can also tell you many things about their personality. If they are seriously toned, you can tell that this man is disciplined; if he's carrying twenty pounds around the middle, you'll know that he's more of a free spirit. Men usually have it so easy taking care of their bodies as young adults that they do not develop good habits for keeping their bodies lean for the long haul.

Body language also speaks volumes in assessing body points. Consider posture: Is he standing straight, shoulders back, or slouching and dragging his feet? Is he compensating for being too tall by hunching over? Are his arms and legs crossed? This is a defensive pose and subconsciously shows that he wants to keep people away. Is he fidgety? This might be a sign that he is a nervous person, especially if he cracks his knuckles, scratches incessantly, or taps his feet. When he walks into a room, does he fade into the woodwork or does he walk in confidently? Are his gestures appropriate or space-invading?

Your preference for body type is completely up to you. However, there are some constants that will apply to the men you'll rate:

Grooming. Personal cleanliness is a must, and details count. Are fingernails manicured or at least cleaned and clipped? What about body odor, perspiration, stinky feet, bad breath? Points can also be taken off when things go too far to the other extreme. You don't want to be eating dinner with someone who is flossing at the dinner table.

Attire. Clothing doesn't have to sport designer logos but it does have to be clean, unwrinkled, fit well, and be appropriate. If he's wearing his best designer T-shirt, jeans, and sport shoes to your best friend's formal wedding, it's not edgy, it's disrespectful.

A MAN'S PERSONALITY

Some men are good at expressing their inner self, but I've found that most are not. Some use humor, charm, or intellect to express themselves. What makes the ideal personality for you is part of your Personal Filter, but what makes a 10 is any man's ability to flawlessly execute that style. Personality is such an important area to rate, especially if you are an older dater. If this guy is not pleasant to be around, it will affect the outcome of every date. At the same time, sweet or funny can raise anyone's score, but don't let his personality con you into doing something you aren't interested in, especially if it's physical.

Renaldy

Sometimes, people with low face and body points will naturally learn to develop strong and engaging personalities. I'm always surprised by how many people will date someone that they are not physically attracted to because they find them to be funny. As an example, Renaldy is an okay-looking guy, okay enough to date regularly. Once, he was in a very informal meeting when a not-so-pretty girl from the temp office next door walked into his office asking for help: she couldn't get her phone to work. Renaldy quickly picked up the phone on his desk and said out loud, "This is the side you speak into, and this is the side you listen to." The girl gave him the double bird and walked away. Renaldy found the shocking gesture hilariously inappropriate. He asked her later that day if he could take her out sometime. Even though he now refers to her as Shrek because she was funny but kind of ogreish, he was swayed at the time by her ludicrous sense of humor.

A MAN'S LIFE SITUATION

Life situation encompasses many things. If a person is a noun, and their face, body, and personality are adjectives, then you can think of their life situation as the verb: it's the way they go about living their life. Where a man lives, who he lives with, what type of work he does, what assets or liabilities he has amassed, his hobbies and interests, his relationships with family and friends, and even the importance he places on his pets all make up a life situation.

Nowadays, there are so many choices for life situations that it has become a huge component of the decision-making process for dating. I took a tour through a Third World country in East Africa and found even among those with so little there are still varying life situations. Even if you are not marriage-minded, the life situations of another will affect not only the way you view that person, but it will affect the time you spend with them. Their life situation will determine how available they are to you, and if they will be able to meet your needs.

For example, dating a guy who tours with a band sounds thrilling, but the reality is that you'll be lonely most nights. Date a guy who owns a chain of chicken restaurants and you will end up talking about (and eating) lots of chicken. Date a guy with kids from a previous marriage, and guess who will be doing their laundry when they come for a weekend?

Men have always felt more pressure to be successful in this area. They are often driven to become a good provider as a measure of success. But just as your body shouldn't define you, do not put extra emphasis on a life situation. It's the same as all the other areas—it's just one aspect of the greater equation. We can be tempted by a great life situation but at the end of the day you are holding hands with a person, not their car. A lux apartment is alluring but when the lights go out it's the man that you're with, not his high-end amenities.

Determining a potential date's life situation is vital because it can alert you to what the quality of a relationship will be. Not only do you need to get the answers to your questions, you need to realize the implications attached to them. For example, if you meet a boating fanatic, you better love fun in the sun. If you're looking for a relationship that will lead to marriage, take points away from a guy's life situation rating if he tells you that he left his last girlfriend when "she got too serious."

The areas to take into consideration are listed below. Feel free to add to this list according to your life situation. Remember, the way you rate the response to these questions is completely personal: all that matters is what you want, what your ideal is, and how close they come to it. Just like you did in chapter 2, use this list to help you clarify what you need and want out of a date.

Marital status. Single, divorced, widowed, separated, married (yikes, is that a red flag or what?)

Children. Does he have children? How many? By how many different partners? If no children, does he want them?

Health issues. Are there any chronic health problems? Does he take care of himself? Does he have health insurance?

Career. Employed? Full time? Part time? Self-employed? Does his job take him away? Salary? Job security?

Finances. How does he handle money? Is there a mortgage, car payment, child support, student loans, credit card debt? Is he generous? Too generous? Too cheap?

Housing. Does he own or rent his home? Does he live alone? With a roommate? Does he live with his parents? Why? How far does he live from you?

Intelligence. Level of education completed (high school, GED, some college, college degree)? Is he naturally smart or clever? (Plenty of successful people do not have college degrees.)

Interests/hobbies. What does he do after work? Athlete or sports fan? Any hobbies? Does he collect anything (art, baseball cards, cars)? How much time does he spend on his interests? How much money is earmarked for his interests?

Family ties. Does he come from a large family or a small family? Where do they live? (This could impact holidays and vacations.) How close is he to them?

Friends. Does he have a lot of friends? Close friends? Friends of the opposite sex? How much time does he spend with them? Does he like your friends? Is he willing to hang out with them?

Spirituality. Is he a member of a formal religion? Does he practice his faith? (People view religious practices differently, even among believers of the same faith, denomination, and even the same place of worship.) Is his religion compatible to yours?

Vices. Does he smoke, do drugs, gamble?

Pets. Does he have any? Does he like animals?

Birthdays and holidays. Does he acknowledge and participate in them?

DO OPPOSITES REALLY ATTRACT?

We are all unique. *The trick is to find someone who brings the same amount to the table as you do—not necessarily the same qualities, but the same amount.* You may have a strength in one area and a weakness in another. Some people want to meet someone who has opposite weaknesses and strengths. Others are drawn to personalities that are similar to the one they have. Some women like to be around someone who agrees with them all the time. Others think a healthy debate is sexy.

As long as you are in the same rating range you should be able to respect the opinion or lack of one from your current dude. When you don't rate in the same range you may feel superior or inferior, regardless of whether you agree on any particular topic. There is a girl out there for every shy guy, and one to respect that debater's opinion, so don't try to fit a square peg in a round hole. Use your Personal Filter and figure out who you want to be with. Then find a guy in your rating range who matches your requirements!

I should also mention that not everyone is ecstatic about their own personality. Take shyness, for instance. Shy people need to work extremely hard to appear outgoing, so they might want to be around someone who is more comfortable being the "front man" in the relationship. If you are good-looking but don't rate yourself with high scores in personality, you might want to be with someone who does have a strong personality. Take the classic supermodel-unattractive rock star couple. I never can figure out this relationship, but it seems to work for many famous duos. Remember, a good-looking shy girl will be in the same range as an average-looking guy with a charismatic personality.

Define Your Perfect Date

Below is a series of opposite personality traits and characteristics. Go through the list once to determine what traits make up your ideal personality for a date, and possibly a mate. Then compare it to the lists you set up for yourself in chapters 2 and 3. Are you finding that you want to be with someone just like you, or someone who is significantly different?

- Supportive, encouraging, a can-do spirit, or a nothing-ever-goes-right attitude, hopeless, or fearful
- Friendly, warm, someone who likes people, or a loner who avoids social situations
- Laughs easily, sometimes, or not at all
- Caring, compassionate, and considerate, or apathetic, doesn't want to get involved
- Cool, level-headed problem solver, or quick to anger, gets upset easily, mopes, whines, and blames others
- Ambitious and passionate, or content to do little
- Outgoing, gregarious, talkative, or quiet, shy, cautious
- Trusting of self and others, or suspicious, envious, jealous
- Confident, or full of self-doubt
- Well-mannered, respectful, or brash, rude, overbearing
- Generous, helpful, or selfish, cheap
- Leader, or follower
- Active, outgoing, or restrained, low energy
- Focused, or scattered

THE WHOLE-MAN

My cousin Tony recently applied for the special forces unit within his branch of the military. He told me about a term he learned called the Whole-Man. The Whole-Man concept is used when new cadets are assessed, and takes into account more than just physical prowess; it also evaluates achievements in academics, leadership, community involvement, as well as personal convictions. In the military, it is assumed that all of the men and women are physically competent soldiers. However, the rest of the criteria are equally important in order to identify who these men and women truly are. It is important information that you can't lie about.

Just as Tony can't ignore the Whole-Man standard, you can't outsmart the Rating Game. While it is human nature to put your best foot forward, you will certainly run across a few men who are willing to put a foot forward that doesn't even belong to them. Without even knowing the Rating Game, these men will try to fake their ratings. But I know how to spot even the best poser. Assessing a man based on the Rating Game will thwart his efforts to pull the wool over your eyes because these wolves are banking on the art of distraction. They have been able to redirect other women with one particularly attractive quality and then hope you will assume that the rest of them lines up in the same great way. The Rating Game forces you to carefully check out all of the areas of their life independently, which will keep them from lying, or at least expose their lies relatively quickly.

A bold-faced lie is usually transparent, but it is those tricky little lies of omission that can snag us. It is like when a man says he has a boat in the marina, but the truth is that his parents had a boat there once when he was five. Use your best detective work to ask the tough questions, and you'll get the most revealing answers. And as I tell my friends, if it looks like a duck and walks like a duck, chances are, you're stuck with a duck.

WHEN TO RE-RATE A LIFE SITUATION

Use the points in the list that follows as conversation starters. A simple question like, "What do you like to do when you're not working?" opens the dialogue and gets you info on their life situation.

However, be aware that more often than not, a person's true life situation is revealed slowly. That handsome, charismatic, funny guy may turn out to be a bad-tempered, spoiled creep. While you can only judge someone based on what you know at the time, it's going to be necessary to rerate the personality and the life situation categories from time to time.

The surface aspects of a life situation can be pretty apparent or can be gleaned from an initial conversation. However, the deeper life situation issues that are just as important, such as how he handles money, health problems, or his spirituality, won't be revealed immediately. People often disclose their true life situations in stages. For example, on a first date he might offer up the basics: what type of work he does, what part of town he lives in, and his favorite free time activity. This basic information might be all you'll get for a while unless you are willing to offer up your vital statistics. Sharing past experiences and thoughts about life will help open up a dialogue, and if you can steer the conversations correctly, you'll find out more of what you need to know.

You can rate several times in the beginning of a relationship, especially for this category. If you sense a large issue in the life situation area in the "getting to know you" stage, you'll still have an easy out. If you see that your relationship is moving toward the commitment stage, then you want to make sure that you understand everything about his life situation, and rate accordingly.

THE DANGERS OF AGE RATING

In our modern age it is a mistake to assume that someone's age factors into their rating. That's because age alone—like any other attribute—cannot determine someone's full worth. Age can be a factor in a person's overall rating, but not always. People are living longer and better. Forty is the new thirty and thirty is the new twenty-one. We look younger, continue active recreation, and live it up well into our senior years.

Don't assume that just because someone is a different age than you he isn't worth rating. Instead, use the Rating Game to discover where he truly rates. Maybe you will be surprised to find that this man has a great body or personality, which will elevate his overall number higher than you would expect. Maybe you will find that even though the person may have fine lines or grown children, he still rates higher overall than you thought. He could even rate higher than you, which would put him out of your range. If you think that just because you are young and have a hard body any middle-aged rich man is going to be happy with you then you could end up being sorely disappointed.

There is nothing wrong with dating outside of your age group as long as that is not the sole reason you are dating the person. It may be tempting at first to find someone to take care of you, or if you've always wanted to be treated like a trophy. However, if the older gent doesn't rate the same as you do, you won't get treated the way you deserve.

Beware of completely inappropriate age dating. This usually happens when people are vulnerable and are pursued by someone who is in an authoritative or powerful position, such as the classic Hugh Hefner–Playboy Bunny relationship. At the same time, beware of get-rich-quick dating strategies. Dating older guys just to advance your career is going to make you feel icky inside and it may take a while to realize it but one day you will and it won't just go away because you break up. And dating guys twenty years younger means you have officially hit cougarhood, proceed with caution.

Paul and Carly

Paul met Carly on an Internet dating site. When he first saw her picture he thought she was beautiful, but he could tell that she was a little older than the women he normally dates. In fact, Carly was almost ten years older than Paul. The two started dating and Paul was impressed with her drive and youthful ambitions. Carly was an instant hit with his friends, and the two quickly became an item.

However, the thrill left pretty soon. Carly made obnoxious remarks about Paul's TV habits, and Paul began to tire of paying for high-priced meals and drinks. Paul's sensitivity grew and he found himself questioning the relationship. We sat down and rated the relationship, which is something that Paul should have done at the beginning. Upon analysis, Paul rated himself a 7, and her an 8. Paul was shocked that she was higher than him and immediately wanted to change his score. He couldn't understand how she could rate higher than him. When he started dating her he loved the fact that she was glamorous and successful, but he thought she would rate lower because she was older. However, even despite her age she was still better-looking and more successful.

DATING IN YOUR RANGE

When you're rating men, you are looking for someone who rates the same whole number as you. The range of daters will be in the decimals. A 5 will be satisfied with anyone from 5.0 to 5.9. A 5.9

should not date a 6. It may seem only a point off but that decimal is the difference between being a top-hitting minor leaguer and squeaking by playing for the majors. Trust me, stick with your whole number and you'll be a lot happier. Or, see if you can improve your rating just the littlest bit to make up for the difference.

Not all numbers are easy to find. There are plenty more 5s out there than 10s or 2s. For example, if you are a 9 it could take you a while to find another 9, but once you find that 9 it will be so worth it. My motto is similar to what they say on the playground. Instead of saying, "Why don't you fight someone your own size?" I say, "Date someone in your own range."

Toni

Toni had been away for a long vacation and went to pick up her mail. This thirty-five-year-old yoga instructor sauntered into the post office, and almost dropped the gum out of her mouth when she saw a tall, handsome man buying stamps. She took a quick glance at his fingers: no wedding ring. Toni did a fast check on her rating. She has a nice

THE REAL ESTATE ANALOGY

I know that people are not houses, but there are some similarities between choosing a guy and choosing a house that we need to consider. Just like a house, someone can be beautiful on the outside and a mess on the inside. A house can also have all the right amenities but be located in the wrong neighborhood, or be available at the wrong time (like, right after you just signed a lease somewhere else).

The process for getting a date can be just as time-consuming as buying a house. First, before you buy a house, you'll want to see all of it. We know what the exterior looks like, but we'll also want to take a peek inside. Likewise, no one buys a house without considering the location and your needs and how this house can fulfill them.

When you are considering becoming involved romantically with a person there should also be consistent factors that are always considered. These include the Rating Game's four categories as seen through your Personal Filter.

face, stretched and toned yoga bod, and she was happy with all the things that were going well in her life. She gave herself an 8 as she waited in line, hoping that this man would notice her.

Which he did! He smiled at her and she smiled back. She noticed that he was waiting for her outside the post office, and he asked her for the time. They began talking, and she got his name. Turns out that Evan was new in town. He just accepted a job at the local YMCA as a tennis pro, but didn't really know his way around. He was engaging and friendly. He looked her in the eye when they talked, even though he was a good six inches taller than her. In just a few minutes, Toni was able to tell that Evan was also an 8, so she agreed to grab a cup of chai tea with him before her next class.

PRACTICE RATING ON YOUR _____

Practice the Rating Game on every single guy you can find. You'll be surprised how the combinations of numbers work together. You'll also learn more about which guys are in your league, and which guys are not.

Here's a list of do's and don'ts for rating guys:

• Do rate yourself before you rate anyone else

• Do rate yourself often, especially before you hit a prime singles spot

• Don't tell him what you rate yourself

- Do rate early and rate often once you start a relationship, especially if you hit a rough patch

- Don't let guys know you are rating them

- Do rate all the single guys you meet

- Don't tell him what you rate him!

THE RATING GAME WORKSHEETS

10 = PERFECTION

9 = THE BEST IN THE ROOM

8 = GREAT

7 = GOOD

6 = ABOVE AVERAGE

5 = AVERAGE

4=OKAY

3 = BELOW AVERAGE

2 = NOT GOOD

1 = CALL SECURITY

Green Light!

Your face is good, his is average, but his body is slightly better. Your personality may be bigger, but his life situation is stronger. The points are slightly different, and come from different places, but the rating averages the same!

EXAMPLE	YOU	HIM
Face	7	5
Body	6	7
Personality	8	6
Life situation	5	7
=	26	25
Divide by 4	6.50	6.25
Rating	6: above average	6: above average

Red Light!

Your face scores are very different, and his body is dramatically better. Your personality and life situation are close but his are still stronger. The points are not even close, and in the end the relationship will reflect the difference.

EXAMPLE	YOU	HIM
Face	6	8
Body	4	7
Personality	7	8
Life situation	6	7

EXAMPLE	YOU	HIM
=	*23*	*30*
Divide by 4	*5.75*	*7.5*
Rating	*5: average*	*7: good*

Now you give it a shot! Rate your face, body, personality, and life situation. Add up your numbers, then divide by 4. I add this up all the time with my cell phone calculator. This is your number and your rating. Now do the same for him. Is it a match?

EXAMPLE	YOU	HIM
Face		
Body		
Personality		
Life situation		
=		
Divide by 4		
Rating		

6.

Reading into the Numbers

PEOPLE ARE AS different as snowflakes, and no two are alike. However, there are some generalizations we can make about snowflakes. For instance, a higher altitude creates a lighter snowflake, warmer conditions will cause an icier snowflake, and acid rain, well, that's no good for snowflakes. The same is true for daters. While everyone is completely unique, there are some generalizations we can make, especially in the realm of behavior. In my years of rating I've found that certain numbers often respond to others in similar ways. And the way certain numbers perceive themselves can also be within a common range.

The following profiles capture typical behaviors and attitudes of the people who rate specific values. Use these guidelines as another insight into the person you've just rated. However, you need to be careful when you are making broad generalizations. Just like all blond girls aren't easy and all football players aren't dumb, there are exceptions to these rules.

4S ARE SELF-AWARE

When you find yourself on the short side of average, you can't really miss your faults. 4s often have a keen sense of self-awareness. 4s are the people who already own a full shelf of self-help books. They realize that they have work to do, and are usually willing to put in the time it takes to improve themselves. Because of this, they often share that truly majestic quality that can only be found in someone who is aware of themselves in deep and meaningful ways. And because they have looked at themselves so analytically, 4s turn out to be very insightful. What's more, they are usually good listeners and give brilliant advice.

The reason 4s are so insightful is because they've been through their own pain, loss, and disappointments. Chances are good that they might still be going through some ordeal. If you can get close enough to them you're likely to find a wound of some sort under the surface. Yet 4s can also laugh at their flaws, and are sometimes morbidly funny. Their dark sense of humor reflects their struggles.

4s tend to be very noncommittal because of their profile dips or depression. 4s will often reach for the unattainable because they don't feel worthy of true happiness, and expect to be rejected. However, their own problems often attract them to other broken people. By default and against their own inclination, 4s typically end up attached to others who struggle with something in life as well. My advice is, a 4 may make an excellent companion if you are going through your own emotional stuff. If you share the same vice, they may offer you the support you need to break your bad habits. Then together, you may be surprised how each one of you can grow and develop into someone better than when you originally met.

Ty

Ty grew up as a scholarship kid at a private school where his mom worked. All of his friends lived in big, fancy houses in a different part of town. Ty's dad was a carpenter, and his family lived in a two-bedroom apartment and drove an old truck. His parents were good people, but they just didn't have much.

Early on at school this income-level disparity didn't matter, but as Ty got older he developed his own set of survival tools and coping mechanisms for trying to fit in. His default response was his humor, and he even found himself making fun of his folks in order to be accepted by his classmates.

By the end of high school, Ty realized that the joke was really on him. Ty's father was a large man, and Ty always assumed that he would have the same physique. But by his eighteenth birthday, Ty's physique more closely resembled his mother's narrow petite frame than his father's hunky build. On top of that, he started losing his hair. Though he never let on to anyone else about his physical disappointments, Ty was devastated. He continued to use humor to deflect his inner hurt, and found himself searching for a relationship with someone who could understand his pain. He ended up with a girl that had a serious dip in her life situation because of a previous bad marriage and bad upbringing. The two shared a dark sense of humor. However, she eventually got over her past and her life situation improved. Then she left Ty and broke his heart.

There are parts of Ty's life that he can never change. However, he has high personality scores: he's got a great sense of humor and is an incredible listener. Now he's seeking someone that rates in his range who he hopes will be able to stick with him for the long term.

5S HAVE THE MOST FUN

5s are the partiers because there are simply more of them. And, if they are happy with where they are in life, they will realize a contentment that comes with being in the mainstream. 5s are one of the most satisfied numbers to be. A 5 is usually under the radar; they aren't in tune with the sometimes exhausting pressure to succeed. The goal in the life of a 5 is to get along. Like a cowboy riding on the range, a 5 is proud of his accomplishments and enjoying the ride. A content 5 offers a comfy heartfelt feeling of acceptance. Because of their large base, 5s also offer a sense of community that supports you and what you have done and become in life.

However, being comfortable with yourself is great, but even contentment requires maintenance. The downside to dating a 5 is contentment's ugly cousin: complacency. Complacency is a disregard for maintaining the areas that led them to be rated as a 5 in the first place. Another trouble with complacency is that when real problems are left unchecked, a 5 can quickly spiral down to a 4, a 3, or less. Lose a job, gain some weight, or experience an emotional upset and before you know it your numbers have slipped way down. If you are a 5 chances are you have already taken most of your worst qualities into account. The good news is that with just a little maintenance you can keep that 5 fueled up and feeling just right.

Maybe this guy will never be a scholar or social butterfly, but to be average is enough for most people. That is why they call it average—because it is where most people are at.

Tracy

Tracy has what she considers an above-average personality, which she rates as a 6. She works hard at everything she does. Her taller, wider frame is not considered a dancer's body (4 in body), but Tracy loves to dance, and does so whenever she can. She takes her responsibilities very seriously and has purpose in her heart to do what's right in every area of her life (personality, 6). This early twenties brunette finished school with high grades, maintained her sexual purity, and is now eager to find love, even though she is living back with her parents in the suburbs (life situation, 5).

Her first encounter with an online dating service brought her face-to-face with a man she felt drawn to. She quickly realized that she and Jack wanted the same things in life. It seems as though they have the same temperament and values. Both are conservative but social. They are both a couple of steps into their careers and headed in the same direction toward a promotion. Tracy had a lot in common with Jack but didn't think his pic made him look like the knight in shining armor she had dreamed of.

I showed Tracy how to rate herself and him. Even with her high moral esteem, she rated herself a 5, deducting a few points for her body. She was comfortable with the rating because she was happy to be considered within the mainstream; she was

Return Policy

With a sales receipt, a full refund in the original form of payment will be issued from any Barnes & Noble store for returns of new and unread books (except textbooks) and unopened music/DVDs/audio made within (i) 14 days of purchase from a Barnes & Noble retail store (except for purchases made by check less than 7 days prior to the date of return) or (ii) 14 days of delivery date for Barnes & Noble.com purchases (except for purchases made via PayPal). A store credit for the purchase price will be issued for (i) purchases made by check less than 7 days prior to the date of return, (ii) when a gift receipt is presented within 60 days of purchase, (iii) textbooks returned with a receipt within 14 days of purchase, or (iv) original purchase was made also glad that she had told Jack the truth about what she looked like.

Then she rated Jack. From what she knew about him, she rated him as a 5 as well. She felt much more confident about meeting him. To test the theory, she quickly rated her boss's son, whom she secretly had a crush on. She rated this young doctor an 8. Just as she suspected, Tracy would not have been happy with the young doctor; she always thought him a bit showy for her taste, even though he was very cute. Tracy was ready to meet Jack because she felt good about herself and his potential rating. A year later, her Internet honey took her down the most romantic memory lane that ended with an engagement ring. Fantastic 5s, finding each other!!

6S ARE CONFIDENT

There is something very uplifting about living above the average, even if only by one point. The confidence of knowing that you are above the crowd is intoxicating. It's like being at a concert and getting to go backstage. Even if you don't get to meet the musicians it still feels like you've got something special. Being above the curve can come naturally or you might have had to work hard at it. In the dating realm confidence is like sirens on a police car, they help you get noticed. However, confidence comes with obligation and responsibility. Like those sirens, confidence is only as good as the badge driving the car.

The downside of being a 6 is arrogance, which can happen when you become overly confident. Being overly confident means you can't deliver what you are presenting. Simply said, 6s can get in over their heads, especially when they fall for an 8; then they'll find that their confidence turns to fluff. It's like walking around with the VIP pass from a concert hanging around your neck. You are not the musician, it is not your show, and chances are you don't work for the band or the concert hall. You most likely got the pass by accident or worked really hard to track one down.

A 6 should be humble because they are really just one point away from average, but I've found that they often get cocky and humble pie turns to pie in the face. At the heart of an overinflated behavior may be a person who doesn't want others to discover who they really are for fear that they won't measure up. But if a 6 considers themselves to be blessed to be above average they'll be happy to find another 6 to date.

6s can also be motivating and interesting, because they are above the norm. My advice: a 6 relationship can be solid, and is worth the effort to find someone who rates the same as you. If you're a 6, don't settle for anything less and don't pretend to be anything more.

Lucas

Lucas comes from a very ambitious and successful family. Each of his siblings is accomplished. Lucas has a host of 6 traits but always had to struggle more than the rest of his family. His pleasing demeanor and air of confidence landed him a spot on his college football team. But as he got older and his talents softened, he realized that it was not long before his team lifestyle would end.

Athletes get a lot of girls, and so did Lucas. He ended up in a long-term relationship with one of the cheerleaders. After years of dating she wanted a commitment, but he was afraid she would figure out how mediocre he really was. Her ultimatum ended their relationship. Unfortunately, he was completely unaware of the mind games he was playing and soon found himself in another relationship where he was once again over his head.

After graduation Lucas had moved from player to assistant coach at the same college. Though he still got the prestige of being around the coaches and the team, Lucas felt the age gap was wider. Now the shenanigans he would have to pull to keep each new flame at bay were traitorously irresponsible. Lucas had hooked up with the new volleyball coach. She was cute and quick-witted, and Lucas felt overwhelmed. To keep her off the trail of his incompetence he would avoid taking her out alone; they mostly hung out at the games where either she was working or he was working.

Lucas got himself caught in a trap that so many 6s fall into. Instead of feeling great that he was above average, he believes that since he is above average he deserves the best. He is able to fake his way into some situations because of his confidence and mild accomplishments, but once he gets in the door he simply can't maintain the status quo.

Instead of looking for the best, Lucas would be better off looking for what would be best for him. If he were with another 6, he would feel like his accomplishments were good enough, and then he could stop the charade and enjoy his life.

7S ARE LOYAL

7s know they have a good thing going, and don't want to stray from it. Many 7s believe they have what it takes to make someone happy. 7s are optimistic and will stick by you no matter what. They see the good in everyone just like they see the good in themselves. A 7 has solid scores that feel very stable. This stability helps them stay loyal and see the good in others around them. 7s are like Hondas: good cars that are reliable, predictable, retain their value, and last forever.

However, some people find predictable to be boring. To add spice to their lives a bored 7 will try to hook up with an 8 to liven things up. In fact, many 7s can steady 8s with their deep loyalty. A 7 often feels like their dependability qualifies them to have whatever they want in life. But if they do succeed in snagging an 8, they will quickly find themselves in over their heads.

The pitfall of being a 7 is that it is easy to assume that their loyalty is enough to create a stable relationship, and this presumption can lead to disaster. A 7 needs to make sure they are not getting abused because of their undying faithfulness. Often, 7s find themselves hanging on to a relationship until the bitter end, even though they realized that they should have jumped ship earlier.

Brenda

Brenda always makes the best out of any situation. At thirty-four, she has a small group of close friends. She feels good about her upscale community, and is thankful that she has a steady job as an engineer at the water plant. She has a nice frame and a pleasant face, but she wonders why she is waiting for the man she adores to really take notice of her.

Brenda has been hanging out with Sean for a couple of years and she still doesn't feel noticed. He invites her to all his parties.

They go out for dinner occasionally, have great conversations, and get along well, but their friendship has plateaued. No sparks.

One night after dinner and a few drinks the two were in her car saying good night. He leaned over to hug her before getting out of the car and that was it. No kiss and no call the next day. She thought for sure that night would take their relationship to the next level, but once again it didn't. She rationalized that Sean was just busy and willing to take their relationship slowly. But the next time he had a party it was clear that Sean had brought a date: he couldn't keep his hands off a particularly beautiful girl.

Brenda was hurt, but like a trusted sidekick, she still hangs on to Sean. She hopes one day he will realize how loyal she is, and what a fantastic girlfriend she would make. Unfortunately, it's clear to everyone else around them that Sean isn't looking at Brenda as a serious contender for his affections.

8S ARE ENTERTAINING

If you are looking for a good time, find an 8 and hold on tight! 8s make you feel like you're part of the action. 8s make things happen and invite everyone in for the fun. An 8 is like a Pied Piper that people are drawn to. Even compared to 10s, 8s are the most coveted rating because they are amazing to be with yet still seem attainable.

Everybody believes that 8s like them and that they honestly stand a chance to date them, even if they don't believe they rate as high. That's one reason why 6s and 7s are always chasing 8s: 8s can make it look like something great is going to happen, and a lot of times it does. But what everyone doesn't realize is that 8s are willing to have fun with anyone, and others often mistake attention for romance or even interest. Eventually an 8 will realize that they are doing all the work in a relationship, regardless of whether they are dating up or down. In fact, 8s are the ones who most often get disappointed with their dates, and they break up with more people than anyone else.

8s are like middle children. They have 9s and 10s above them and 7s and 6s below. With so many numbers that are close by to choose from, I find that 8s instantly connect with 6s but eventually it becomes apparent that the 6 is not bringing the same amount to the table. On the other hand, 8s are also drawn to 9s because of their charisma. 9s love to hang out with 8s because they're fun and they make them look good. But in the end, 9s want to date other 9s.

D.J.

D.J. is always the life of the party. Not only is he tall and good-looking, he's got a smile that goes all the way across his face, and a personality to match it. Born on a farm, D.J. is a natural performer and hit the ground running when he moved to Hollywood. He met a drop of sunshine at a concert last year who turned out to be a performer as well. D.J. thought he had met his soul mate. Cara was everything and he loved her. The two dated for almost a year and he was sure that he would spend the rest of his life with the most amazing girl he had ever met.

One day, seemingly out of nowhere, D.J.'s perfect catch told him that she wanted a break. D.J. was confused. All he could think about was how much fun they had together and how much he adored her. In hindsight he recalled Cara's disdain for his meager upbringing. She had been raised by wealthy celebrity parents and she didn't understand his need to return to the farm to be with his family. She had also commented on his social status. It took D.J. ten days and constant replaying of one amazing breakup anthem to realize Cara would never be happy with him over the long run. He broke off the relationship entirely. Now he's free to date another 8 who will find his upbringing a unique part of his total package.

9S ARE EXCLUSIVE

It can be lonely when you are at the top, but meeting another 9 is worth the wait. Being a 9 is like having four aces in a poker game. And let me tell you, there are a host of perks that come with being at the top. Being with a 9 is like hanging out with a celebrity: you get the best table at restaurants, and waiters are actually pleasant to you. Shopping turns into a breeze instead of a chore, and you'll find your bags filled with VIP passes and complimentary items.

So it should be no surprise that 9s quickly become accustomed to the privileges of being coveted. Unfortunately, this can lead to arrogance and spoiled behavior, especially if their parents always treated them like a special child. This conditioning makes dating one of these grown-up monsters about as pleasant as sticking your head in a lion's den, unless you can either see beyond the pretense, or completely relate because you are a 9 yourself. The sad thing is that 9s lose personality points when they act snooty and risk losing the very status that exalted them.

There are not a ton of 9s around, and finding one that isn't dedicated to keeping up appearances is even rarer. However, if you are a 9, you'll find that others are actually magnetically drawn to you. You will be the prize they have been seeking, because your 9ness adds to their stature. Sometimes a 9 will seek someone who is just a 9 in a single category, mistaking them for an overall 9 rating. In other words, a 9 might only want to date Ivy League graduates, but as we know, one attribute does not define a person. My advice: be patient, and 9s will come.

Charlie

Charlie grew up in a high-profile family in his Midwestern city. He and his brothers were all considered the best-looking, most talented, and most popular kids at their schools. Charlie excelled in sports and was even a corporately sponsored snowboarder in high school. Charlie's parents thought their handsome son's privileged life was a testament to their hard work and a blessing from above. They indulged him in ways that were well intentioned: they bought him a new car every year after he turned sixteen and made sure every article of clothing he wore had the very best label.

At the age of twenty-two Charlie moved out to the East Coast and set himself up for success in a trendy apartment in Manhattan. His best friend from high school had made a name for himself as a local reporter, giving Charlie entrée into the hottest nightspots in town. Though everyone thought he was a bit arrogant, one could not deny that for the most part Charlie had it all: a great personality, stunning looks, and a lifestyle to match.

A short while later he met a high-society girl from a wealthy family. He attended a couple of her parties and quickly found himself hooked on her. Charlie became part of her entourage. He thought that her money, fame, and talent all spelled success. Unfortunately, this girl's nervous breakdown, legal troubles, and whacky behavior really equaled a train wreck.

Now that the debris has cleared, Charlie left the Big Apple for a bit to regroup. His lesson was learned the hard way: it takes more than a 10 in one area to equal a 9!

PERFECT 10S

As I've said before, true perfection is even rarer than meeting a 1, 2, or 3. If you meet a perfect 10 you may have truly died and gone to heaven. If you're not old enough to remember Bo Derek in the movie *10*, go out and rent it, just for the scene of her running on the beach. If you really believe that you've met a 10, go ahead and pinch yourself to see if you're dreaming. I believe that it's possible to meet a 10, but their rating might be fleeting. We all have flaws that come out sooner or later. And all it takes is one flaw in one area to fall off the 10 pedestal. My advice: if you think you're a 10 in every area, you are one very lucky, but potentially very lonely girl. Self-esteem is a great thing, but honesty is a better policy.

1S, 2S, OR 3S

An overall rating of 1, 2, or 3 is actually very hard to achieve because most people have at least a couple of average qualities—or one better-than-average—that will increase the lowest scores in other areas. Even Charles Manson has an average body. However, if you truly rank someone in these ranges, they are probably not best suited to be dating, even if you hold yourself to this same level of low esteem. To score this low in all areas indicates that this man does not deserve more consideration from you. If you truly believe that your score is this low, you might consider professional psychological help, or review again chapter 4, and seriously consider doing the work to increase your score.

If you do connect with a 1, 2, or 3, beware of the project that you are taking on. I can guarantee that you'll evaluate this guy as a "fixer-upper." But don't let your generous spirit and your best intentions guide your dating life. This isn't the Peace Corps. A 1, 2, or 3 will hold on to you like a drowning man, and may eventually succeed in pulling you under. This person doesn't have enough self-awareness to realize how destructive they can be for others. My advice is, get them professional help and get going in the other direction.

EVEN MORE ON MODERATES, SPIKES, AND DIPS

In any league there are different players and different positions. *You can date anyone that rates in the same league as you but just like there are different positions on a team there are different ways to get your numbers in the Rating Game.* The more frequently you rate others, the better you'll get at distinguishing how you interact with different combinations of the averaged rating. Because we are made up of the sum of our parts, you might find that you are attracted to a strong personality, and not quite as concerned about a specific face or body type. Or, you may be honestly attracted to a life situation: nothing wrong with that. You are compatible with anyone in your number range but will have different experiences with people who achieve their total score in different ways.

Once you've found someone who rates within your range, take a fast look at the values of each of the four categories. Because it is crucial that you stay in your number range, if your Personal Filter requires greatness (that is, 8, 9, or 10 ratings) in a certain area, you need to make sure that the rest of the numbers can create an average number that matches yours. A spike will work in your favor in this situation, and you might have to sacrifice the other areas for a hit. If you are a 6 and want to date someone who's really attractive, you are going to want to find someone who has a spike in face but lower numbers in the other areas so that they are still a 6. And if you're a 7 and you really get turned on by a weight lifter's body, you'll have to be able to live with a guy whose other areas rate lower.

When looking at the individual numbers, see if the numbers are moderately within a range (up or down by a point), completely even across the board, or if they spike or dip. The same rules apply for men with spikes and dips as they did for you. Read through these descriptions to learn more about these patterns.

MODERATES

When someone has similar numbers in all four areas they are considered moderate. Moderate numbers could look like 4-5-4-6 or 7-7-6-8. Moderate numbers will only vary within one point from area to area. Moderate numbers reflect an overall balanced person, no matter what the averaged number reflects. In any rating range, it is very likely that the vast majority of men you will meet are moderates. Moderates offer the fewest surprises when dating, and as Martha Stewart says, that is a good thing.

Link Up and Expect
• Moderate with moderate: an even-keeled, conventional relationship

• Moderate with spike: impressive, inspiring, exciting dates

• Moderate with dip: a profound, reflective, edgy relationship

SPIKES

A spike has one amazing number that they know will get them lots of attention. A spike would vary from the lowest number by at least 4 points like 4-5-4-8 or 6-10-7-7. Spikes are generally positive people. Like a team with one amazing player, spikes realize that they have a ringer feature. Spikes love dips because they can relate to them in an opposite kind of way. Spikes might be looking for an ace in every relationship because they have one themselves.

Link Up and Expect
• Spike with spike: spirited, competitive, lots of challenging energy

• Spike with moderate: supporting, sustaining, feel like they are deeply admired

• Spike with dip: contrasting, synergy, yin yang in rare form

DIPS

When a person scores lower in one area, and sometimes even in two areas, that is considered to be a dip. A dip has one number that is below the others by more than 3 points, like 7-6-7-4 or 5-2-5-6. A dip can mean several things. Dips tend to love moderate raters because they always have something they are missing: a complete package. Even numbered raters can be comforting for a dip. A dip can appreciate a spike because they sense the other's uniqueness, and can relate to the psychology that accompanies that rating.

Dips can indicate a problem area, or signal unhappiness about some aspect of life, but not always. Sometimes, it is interesting to see how people compensate for their weak attributes, which often make them stronger overall. The key is to get a sense of if the person is content with having a dip or if they are down on their dip. Remember Jesse Billauer's story in chapter 4. He is a paraplegic that has made peace with the dip in his body. He is making the most of the incredible attributes he has in the three other areas.

If someone is truly unhappy with their dip, they will be extremely melancholy, which some people like. If a person thinks that they can change a negative area in their life, chances are they will be successful doing so. Then you'll have to see if you can keep up with their new rating. However, if they are content with their dip but you expect change, you're the one who will be disappointed. Proceed with caution if you find yourself dating someone who is down on their dip. However, if you are down on your dip, do something about it before it becomes a bigger issue in your life.

Link Up and Expect
- Dip with dip: acceptance, accommodating, patience

- Dip with moderate: compassion, caring, receptive

- Dip with spike: exciting, stirring, rousing

Hugo

Hugo and Chrissy were introduced through a mutual friend. Hugo is nine years into an IT job that is somewhat stagnant. He lives in a modest home that he and his sister inherited. His involvement with Chrissy started with a phone call that turned into a double date. Chrissy is a graphic designer who has a lot of talent but not a lot of opportunity.

The two had so much fun on their first date that Chrissy agreed to see Hugo again. At first they had long chats on the phone but then Hugo noticed that Chrissy seemed uninterested and less available. She ended up blowing him off altogether. Hugo turned to the Rating Game for help. This is what the numbers said:

	Hugo	Chrissy
Face	7	8
Body	7	8
Personality	8	5
Life situation	5	4
OVERALL=	6.75	6.25

As you can see, their overall numbers match, which is probably why their mutual friend thought they would be good together. Unfortunately, they both had strong dips in their life situation points. Hugo wasn't thrilled with his life situation, but he didn't want to change it. At the same time, Chrissy is very down on her dip. Chrissy thought she would be designing Web sites for trendy loft apartments by now. She imagined her life so differently than it currently is and longs for what she wishes it could be. Chrissy was disheartened by her own life, and wasn't satisfied with Hugo either, even though they were in the same range. Being down on your dip is a major faux pas, and can actually bring your personality scores down. For example, after learning about Chrissy's disappointment with her life and how it was affecting her, Hugo rerated her personality a 3, which brought her overall score down to a 5.75, and which was no longer compatible to his score. Bottom line: if you notice that someone is down on their dip then quickly take that into consideration. Even if you like melancholy, be careful that you don't end up cleaning up someone else's messy life.

Chelsea

Chelsea was just nineteen when she transferred to a new college in the middle of her sophomore year. She walked into her new English class the first day, and noticed a shy young man sitting behind her. She learned that his name was Taylor, and Chelsea thought Taylor's tattoos and funky hair were so cute. Later in the day Chelsea noticed that Taylor was also in her Spanish class, and she made a point of sitting near him. Soon the two were talking, and became fast friends. About six months later they began calling each other boyfriend and girlfriend.

Chelsea came from an unstable family who could not afford to keep her at this new school. Taylor's family lived near the campus, and they offered to house Chelsea to cut her living expenses. While living with her boyfriend's family was not the best option, Chelsea didn't know what else to do. She felt that they were too young to get married, and because she didn't have any money, she believed that she didn't deserve marriage, especially to a great guy like Taylor.

I helped Chelsea run her numbers and they looked like this:

	Chelsea	Taylor
Face	7	8
Body	6	7
Personality	8	6
Life situation	3	6
OVERALL=	6	6.75

Even though the two are in the same range, Taylor is a moderate and Chelsea is a dip. Her numbers were relatively constant except for her life situation. We looked at her math more closely. I showed Chelsea that if she raised her life situation points by 3, she would still match Taylor. Or, if the two got married, Chelsea might adopt his life situation points, and the two would still match. However, if they kept the numbers exactly the way they are now, Chelsea may get depressed about the life situation and begin to feel worse about herself, and perhaps sabotage her personality points and/or ruin the relationship.

Chelsea and I brainstormed on how she could increase her life points. One solution was for her to get a part-time job. That way, she would be able to stay at school and ease the financial burden her parents were feeling. With the extra money she earned, Chelsea would be able to afford campus housing, and she would not have to live with Taylor's family. That would certainly save their relationship until they were really old enough to get married.

Dips can create a fragility, so even if your numbers jive, don't be afraid to take a deeper look. It is still possible that you will find a way to ensure the relationship doesn't take a bad turn later.

TRANSFERENCE

Our numbers are, for the most part, our numbers. We can't give them away, or pass them on to someone else, no matter how we try. For example, your face rating doesn't affect the rating of the guy walking by you with his so-cute new puppy. His dog might

DESCRIBE RATINGS WITH ADJECTIVES

Adjectives can help you explain spikes or dips. The person who has a spike in face but scores 6 overall could be called "an attractive 6," or the person who has a great body but scores a 5 overall could be called "a hot 5." If someone is a 7 across the board you could call them "a solid 7." Use adjectives to help you pinpoint how you arrived at their rating or where they spike or dip.

be cute, but just because he's looking at you doesn't make him cuter. Wish as I might the same is true for body points, I'm stuck with mine unless I start a new and drastic exercise program. I have always been bottom-heavy and my close friend is top-heavy. We always thought if we could just share these attributes we would both be perfect. (Beer goggles are an entirely different story.)

Personalities can be imitated, but your personality can't really "rub off" onto someone else. If you meet a guy at a bar, he might enjoy your company, or you might bring out his sarcastic wit, but your personality is uniquely your own. Remember, imitation is the most sincere form of flattery.

However, one's life situation can actually be transferred to another. One dater can expose another to better restaurants, the arts, or horror movies. If a relationship progresses into a heavy commitment, there might be talk about moving into the "better" home or apartment and getting rid of all the "bad" furniture. And when we're talking marriage, that's when the LS numbers really move in a drastic and hopefully permanent way.

When we exchange vows with someone we are also exchanging our life situations: both the good and the bad. This can work to your advantage or against you. For some this opportunity to share their most prized attribute is thrilling; for others, this occurrence is maddening. Just as you can transfer your elite connections and three-car garage, you can also transfer your school loans and dysfunctional family members.

Transference should be thoroughly considered if you calculate a spike or dip in the life situation area for the person you are rating. The worst problems I've seen with transference occur when a girl dips in life situation and at the same time, the man spikes in life situation. Words like "gold digger" and "sugar daddy" should come to mind.

Let's say Sue has a 9 face, 9 body, 5 personality, 4 life situation, which equals 6.75. Craig scores 5 face, 5 body, 6 personality, 10 life situation, which equals 6.50. Though their numbers are both 6s, if they get hot and heavy then his 10 life situation number is transferred to her. Now Sue's numbers just went up to 9-9-5-10. She starts thinking that she's a real winner and may soon find herself wondering what she's doing with him. She is a hot 8 and he is a rich 6; if he's foolish enough to give her a credit card there's even a chance that she could mishandle their money, thereby transferring her original lower life situation to him.

Many wealthy singles are trying to combat transference legally. It's the dreaded *P* word, "prenuptial agreement." I've heard many an engaged couple say that they get prenups because they are trying to be logical about their relationships, but in reality they are trying to protect their life situations. This document can bring up all kinds of issues. It intimidates some couples to the point of breaking up, while others see it as a necessary business transaction. While I'm getting a little ahead of myself here (we're supposed to be focusing on dating, not marriage), the point here is that you have to take all aspects of a life situation into consideration before you get too involved.

I remember the first time I saw Eddie Murphy's stand-up act. He was so verbose in his exclamation of "half." He acts as if sharing is the fatal flaw of marriage. There are really only two fatal flaws in a marriage. The first is to enter a marriage with the express intent of keeping part of yourself from your spouse. The second is when your sole interest is in getting part of someone else's stuff. My advice is to stay true to the intentions of dating: it's about giving *and* receiving. If you use the Rating Game and are open and honest, you will ultimately be matched with a person who shares your same values.

CELEBRITY RATINGS

It's fun to see how the Rating Game plays out with the rich and famous. These stars would be considered the highest 9s by most people's standards. However, Hollywood insiders have a different perspective, because everyone in Hollywood has had at least fifteen minutes of fame. Most have VIP access and closets full of designer clothes. To the average person one movie star is the same as any other, but within the biz there are degrees in all four of the rating areas to measure.

Most celebs rate themselves with a different set of highs and lows than ours. It's like looking at the highest-priced shirt at the mall and looking at the highest-priced shirt on Rodeo Drive. They are totally different scales. When we peek into the scales of the elite we see they rate themselves with the same compilation of moderates, dips, and spikes. This is a speculation of how these stars rate, according to how these relationships are reported in the media.

MODERATES

Jennifer Aniston. Jen puts the A in A-lister. Jen has extremely high numbers overall, making her a moderate that's near perfection.

Matt Damon. This star made the most out of every area that he was born with. Though his *Good Will Hunting* counterpart and best friend Ben Affleck has flashier numbers in certain areas, Matt's got more consistency overall.

Jennifer Garner. She is the girl next door who lacks nothing. Though she's not throwing 10s, she still scores evenly.

Kate Hudson. Actress Goldie Hawn's beautiful daughter does not take advantage of her celebrity birthright: she is a star on her own. She has high numbers that are even across the board.

Justin Timberlake. He's bringing his total package back. It is more than luck and life situations that brought his golden locks center stage. Justin pulls high numbers in all the areas. Moderate numbers are a rare find for a musician but his are golden nonetheless.

Luke Wilson. While his celebrity brother Owen rates higher than him overall, Luke's numbers are more consistent.

SPIKES

Drew Barrymore. She started a firestorm with a personality that still burns. We have seen Drew go through many changes since she came on the scene in the 1980s, but the *Never Been Kissed* star is known for her personality. It is because she is down-to-earth in the other areas that she is so believable in the roles she plays.

Jessica Biel. She has a serious 10 body, but not much going on in the other areas. She grew up onscreen and grew into a body that no one saw coming. It's not that she doesn't score well in her other areas, it's just that she scores so high in body that it spikes.

Sean John Combs. He is eccentric and over-the-top. This lyrical genius scores well in the other areas but certainly spikes in personality.

Cameron Diaz. Her long and lean body is her calling card. It's a rare look and it's what she's known for.

Benji Madden. Taking a cue from his twin bro Joel Madden, this background vocalist and guitarist has a similar spike in talent or personality.

Joel Madden. Rockers are frequently spikes in talent or personality. This rocker certainly does not have buns of steel.

Nicole Richie. She used her silver spoon to catapult into our lives. This party girl used her connections to have more than a simple life. By making BFF with the beautiful and always being at the right party on the right night she has parlayed herself into a spiked celebutant.

Britney Spears. She made it big for her ability to make a schoolgirl skirt hot. We were all shocked when her spike waned to reveal how low all of her other numbers really are.

Vince Vaughn. He's a fast-talker with a huge personality. He has boogied his way into our lives on numerous occasions, but it is not his looks that get him into the high life. Vince has a personality that is bigger than his six-five frame.

DIPS

Ben Affleck. This square-jawed talent gets his paycheck for his looks but dips in personality. His cockiness and his vices have always pulled down his scores.

Paris Hilton. Seems content with a simple personality. The Barbieish celebutant has never seemed to be down on her dip. Unfortunately it has kept her in a certain range where dating is concerned.

Brad Pitt. He was never known for his personality but his looks are legendary. Not one to be down on his dip, the Pitt seems to view his other attributes as having three aces in the hole. He acts more like a spike than a dip.

Owen Wilson. A strong vice can be a major dip in personality. Owen scores so high in most areas that it's a shame he loses points because of his pain. The relationship between him and brother Luke goes to show you that siblings can be so different. While Luke was setting track records in school, Owen was getting suspended.

WHEN CELEBS DATE, THEY SHOULD RATE

Look what disasters we could have prevented, and saved all of us double takes at the celeb drama in the checkout lane. The Rating Game can benefit even those who look like they have it all. We all saw these big-time breakups go down, now see what the numbers have to say about it.

GUESS WHO'S DATING DOWN?

Jen Aniston and Brad Pitt. It seemed at the time that this Hollywood "It" couple had it all. Though they looked perfect on the red carpet, their relationship was a classic example of not adding up all the numbers. Jen scores high overall while Brad dips in personality, proving that looks aren't everything and neither is life situation. Jen was so dating down and I'm sure that she saw his dip in character long before we did.

Drew Barrymore and Luke Wilson. Luke was dating down because he was enamored of Drew's personality (which is usually what girls do). Even though Drew is quite a catch, in the Rating Game Luke scores higher in overall points whereas Drew spikes in personality. In the end it usually takes a bit more than bubbling charm to stay enamored.

Paris Hilton and Benji Madden. There are few thrills in the world that compare to dating your BFF's boyfriend's brother. My mother married her BFF's brother. However, the double dates and family vacas can only make up part of your time. The other time is spent in a relationship with just the two of you. Paris rates extremely high in face, body, and life situation whereas Benji has a spike in personality. It is easy to see why Paris would think Benji fills in where she falls short but in the end she brings way more to the table than him and is dating down.

Kate Hudson and Chris Robinson. Kate dated down when she met this rocker who seemed almost famous. Kate's Personal Filter would have her gazing starry-eyed at the long-haired rocker, but in the end Kate scores high overall while Chris just spikes in talent, which is in personality.

Justin Timberlake and Britney Spears, Cameron Diaz, or Jessica Biel. Whether it's Spears, Diaz, or Biel, Justin's always in sync with the hot bods. This total package scores high overall but constantly finds himself dating down with girls who spike in body. Not that these girls aren't fabulous, it's just that in the world of perfect hair, excellent bone structure, hard bodies, charisma, and yachts even a slight dip can elevate one person's number above the other. Justin makes it a habit to stay in a relationship but when he dates down they all end the same way.

GUESS WHO'S DATING UP?

Jennifer Aniston and Vince Vaughn. He's a heck of a rebound but nevertheless Vince Vaughn was seriously dating up when he snagged Jennifer Aniston. Vince did what a lot of guys that have one great attribute do. He used his awesome personality to get a girl who rates as high as his highest number, but when you do the math Vince should have realized that he was in over his head.

Kate Hudson and Owen Wilson. With so much to offer, it is a shame that Owen is dating up. This golden duo looked to be the perfect couple, but Kate's numbers are sunshine all the way across and Owen's just don't add up as high.

Jennifer Lopez and Sean Combs. Combs was definitely dating up with J.Lo, who began a string of dating downs when she dated the then "Puff Daddy." J.Lo scores high across the board but takes a dip in one area, and Combs is just the opposite. He spikes in personality but scores low in the other areas, especially the one where he takes a gun into a nightclub. Combs is a mastermind at using his personality as his ace in the hole, but his bling life situation was more than J.Lo could stand.

PERFECT COUPLES WITH SCORES TO MATCH

Jennifer Garner and Ben Affleck. Ben has a tendency to surround himself with moderates. His best friend, brother, and now wife all have even numbers across the board. Though he scores really high in his other areas his dip in personality drops him into Jennifer Garner's range.

Angelina Jolie and Brad Pitt. A match made in . . . well made nonetheless. This globe-trotting couple's numbers match, but this one is complicated, to say the least. When they met their numbers matched because Angie was a dip in personality and so was Brad. This is where it gets complicated. Immediately after filming *Mr. and Mrs. Smith* Angie's borderline frame became stick-thin: this dropped her points even further. This couple is working through their number discrepancy, and so far so good.

Nicole Richie and Joel Madden. Two peas in a pod. This relationship works because their numbers are in the same range. Nicole spikes in life situation and Joel spikes in personality. They both have a combination of mediocre points with one area spiking. A word of caution to this hot Hollywood couple: a new baby will no doubt force any relationship to go through changes. If Nicole starts racking up points by being Mrs. Mom and Joel continues to be a partying rocker the numbers may change in a way that edges Nicole out of Joel's range.

FLASHBACK: RATING PAST RELATIONSHIPS

We all have had relationships or almost relationships that didn't work and we don't know why. Here is your chance to run the numbers and finally figure it out. You can use the Rating Game to go back and decipher exactly what went wrong. Rate yourself and your beau at that time. Your scores will reveal a lot about how the relationship ended. If you broke up with him chances are you rated higher than him and you were dating down. If he broke up with you then he rated higher and you were dating up.

Jeffrey

Jeffrey is the type of guy that always wants to do the honorable thing. He doesn't kiss-and-tell; as a matter of fact he rarely kisses at all. He adores women but he doesn't want to feel like he's taking advantage of them. So he won't get physical unless he's in a serious relationship, and he's decided that he won't go all the way until he gets married. The problem is that Jeffrey doesn't want to settle down with any of the girls he knows. He met Beth Anne at church and was jazzed about her and invited her to all the church functions, but in the end the two simply remained friends. Currently Jeffrey is seeing Jessica. She is a tempting teacher who now lives in another state. The two call each other often, but don't get to see much of each other.

Jeffrey has always rated himself a 7.75 and his darling girls typically rate the same. So why hasn't Mr. J. been able to find the love of his life? The problem turns out to be sweet Melissa. Melissa was Jeffrey's first love. They were sixteen and Jeffrey thought the world of her. He rated her lovely sixteen-year-old face a 10, her pubescent body a 10, her personality a 9, and her life situation an 8 (big house, good grades, and a great family). He remembers Melissa as a saint.

Going back to the numbers it's easy to see why Melissa left Jeffrey before the winter formal. What is sad is that poor Jeffrey has been waiting for another 9.25 to come along and steal his heart. What the mid-thirty-year-old crooner needs to do is date within his range, and not above it. He needs to really invest in one of the many beautiful bubbly 7.5s that have offered him their heart.

Zack

Zack's story starts off at a lunch with a couple of his female coworkers. Being in the radio biz in Washington State kind of makes you a big deal. Being a sports model in any state makes you a big deal. Zack was both, so when he looked up and saw the most beautiful girl he had ever seen, he felt like she should be his. He knew right away that he wanted this gorgeous waitress and that he was not leaving lunch without some connection. He went to the bathroom to regain his composure and check himself out in the mirror. When he returned to his table his female companions said that they spoke with this hot mystery girl and told her that Zack would be asking for her number.

Zack welcomed the prep work and immediately approached her. He was so overwhelmed by her beauty that he could barely speak. He managed to mumble a few sentences, none of which made sense, but eventually he got her phone number. Zack wasted no time and called Cassie that night, and the two quickly began to see each other.

At twenty-five, Zack's career was really taking off. However, the nineteen-year-old cashier was feeling insecure about life. Cassie was not college-bound and had recently broken up with her high school sweetheart. Zack tried to make Cassie feel secure. He constantly told her how beautiful she was and hoped that validation would settle her. A few months went by and her ex-boyfriend was getting more and more jealous of their relationship. Zack received a threatening phone call from the jealous ex saying he was in for a beating and to leave Cassie alone.

Not only was the ex-boyfriend threatening Zack, he was simultaneously making big promises to Cassie. Zack told Cassie he wanted to marry her but Cassie said that she was going to return to her ex. For the next two years Cassie would sneak dates with Zack and tell him she was confused about her feelings for him and her ex. Eventually Zack's career would take him to Los Angeles. He never saw Cassie again.

To this day Zack thinks about the beautiful girl that broke his heart in Washington. He never understood why she would pick a knucklehead like her unattractive loser ex over him. He knew all along that he was the better catch, and it drove him crazy for years. But a quick tally of the numbers said it all. Zack can now see that back then, he rated himself an 8, while Cassie's beauty pulled up her low life situation and left her with a score of 7. Even though she appreciated Zack's attention, no amount of compliments would ever make a 7 feel secure with an 8.

Then, Zack rated the ex at a 3.5. He still couldn't understand why anyone would go for a 3 over his 8. But Cassie knew that her ex loved all of her, even though she really never loved him. Zack didn't have the foresight to realize that he just wanted her for superficial reasons. But Cassie was afraid that she could never be enough to make Zack happy.

TURNING HEARTACHE INTO HOMEWORK

Can you figure out the lesson that was hidden in your past? Can you now be a better person and a better lover? I hope you figured out earlier that you could never have changed him or protected him from getting hurt. If he feels half the hurt you feel he will have suffered enough.

I have an uncle who rides a motorcycle and was always a straight shooter. He once told me something I never forgot. With his wispy beard and his best intentions he said, "Don't ever get into something you can't wash off with soap and water." I laugh about all the meanings this phrase could have, but I know what he is trying to say: there are many relationships that we get ourselves into that we wish we could get out of as easily as washing our hands.

When we share our heart with someone it can take great effort to get it back. That is why I think it is so important to use the Rating Game, which gives you the best chance at finding a relationship that you will be happy with. But if you have already given your heart to the wrong person and are trying to make a clean break, then it is time to turn your heartache into productive homework. Journaling, writing poems, or talking it over with an obliging ear can help you get on with your life.

Talia

Talia broke up with Darrell after seven months of empty promises and letdowns. There were things about Darrell she liked but she spent most of her time nursing her wounds. She kept telling herself how great it would be if he would keep his word. Ultimately when she rated him he scored low in personality and life situation. She told him that it was over and moved on.

Two months later Darrell gave her a call. Talia had been missing him and was happy to hear from him. Within days the two were back together, but his old flaws would soon follow. The promises fell to the floor again and Talia broke off in a huff. Sadly, this cycle continued through the rest of the year. Each time it took Talia two months to quit thinking of him. As time went by she would feel a little better every day, but Darrell felt worse, until it got so bad that he would call her again. Talia felt better because she knew she had done the right thing and kept her boundaries. Darrell felt worse because he couldn't have her and because he knew he did wrong in the relationship.

To finally get over Darrell and put this cycle to an end, Talia wrote a Japanese poem called a senryu, which is a seventeen-syllable poem similar to a haiku. Now each time she reads her work it strengthens her resolve to let Darrell go once and for all.

Ter-ri-ble cy-cle
Want-ed to be to-ge-ther
Was not very cle-ver

7.

The Rating Game Road Trip

A man gets rejected by the girl he chooses to approach,
but a girl gets rejected by every guy who doesn't approach her.

—REBA

ONCE YOU CAN work the Rating Game, you'll find that meeting men and rating them is almost effortless. Even if you're out of practice, you'll be able to rate the men around you every day. All of a sudden, every single man around you is a potential date, including the guys in your neighborhood, the men at your place of worship, or even the salesmen in your favorite stores. The Rating Game allows you to widen your dating opportunities because the premise is that anyone is datable if they match your score and pass through your Personal Filter.

To begin rating often, you have to throw out some of the old rules of dating. First of all, you can't wait until some guy comes up to talk to you. That strategy went out with the Cadillac Cimarron. It's a new century, and you're going to have to make the first move. The first move for you is to position yourself to be seen and approached.

Every woman's approach to meeting men will be different. Most of the time, your style will be based on your personality. That's why some women seem like they are a male magnet: they have the ability to appear open and willing to talk to anyone, and men respond in kind. It definitely helps to have an upbeat, open, and positive attitude when you are looking for dates, but if that isn't your personality, don't sweat it. I've got great tips in store to make it easier for even the shyest woman on the planet.

No matter what your personality is like, meeting a guy is not about trying to be someone you're not. If you are going to assess someone else's face, body, personality, and life situation, you had better be prepared to show your true self. The Rating Game is like playing an open-handed round of the children's card game Go Fish: you must show all your cards so that you can see if there is a match. The goal is to give any guy a great reason to get to know more about you.

I've determined that there are four basic types of women when it comes to dating: outgoing, flirty, reserved, or cerebral. Read the descriptions that follow and see where you fall. Then I'll show you where the best places to meet men will be so that you can rate the most men to find your match.

OUTGOING

Having an open and outgoing personality is by far the best choice for meeting new people, especially men. If you are outgoing then you already know that you love to talk to new people and are comfortable being in a variety of situations. You have a lot to say and like to keep the conversation moving. Being a sociable person is a real plus when it comes to being inviting and appearing open for conversation. This makes you seem approachable to men, who will find you less intimidating than someone who is more reserved.

Outgoing people often have to learn how to turn it down a notch so that they are not dominating every dialogue. By talking too much you risk a verbal explosion that men really do find overwhelming. Not to mention the fact that if you don't let him speak, you'll miss the opportunity to get to know him, and rate him. My advice to Ms. Gregarious is to let your mucho personality shine for the first ninety seconds and then shut your mouth and listen. Let him get a word or two or he will quickly walk away.

Great places for you to meet men are everywhere! If you can talk your way out of a paper bag, then start at the grocery store and work your way over to Starbucks and hang out there for a while. You can talk to everyone and anyone, so don't hold back. Keep rating as you keep talking, and you'll find that there are men just for you everywhere you turn.

FLIRTY

Flirty is a totally different personality type than outgoing. Outgoing is more about putting your personality out there, whereas flirty is more about luring other personalities toward you. Most flirty people can flirt with men or women, with different motivations. If you are flirty then a smile and a head turn may be all that it takes for you to get anyone to start a conversation: you might already know that meeting men is your forte.

The problem with flirty people is that they must deliver on the promise: once you start the "come hither" signal then you have to show that you are more than a smile and a nod. Your goal is to display more of yourself quickly or you will be just another pretty face at the bar. My advice for Ms. Come Closer is to have an icebreaker ready that showcases your personality. For example, when a man approaches you, you can say, "It's so noisy in here. It reminds me of Texas Tech where I went to school." Bringing up a part of yourself that has substance is a great strategy to parlay your flirty personality into a fast, yet meaningful conversation.

RESERVED

Many reserved women believe that they have the hardest time meeting guys, but this doesn't have to be the case. Being reserved means that you shy away from giving men overt signals to approach you. But it doesn't have to mean that guys won't approach you. Many guys like the challenge of getting past an obstacle. And since meeting guys is not about changing yourself there are ways to use your reserve to work for you.

If you believe, or others have told you, that you are unapproachable, my advice to Ms. Standoffish is to use the "approach and hover" technique. This style is used unconsciously by kids on a playground every day. If you watch them carefully, you'll see that one kid simply moves into the vicinity of another child and continues to play his own game. You don't have to give a certain look or say a word, just hover. This ensures that even the shyest guy will have the opportunity to take on the demure girl challenge. However, once you've got someone's interest piqued, be prepared to keep a conversation going. You need to engage at least long enough to rate them, and then if they are not a match, pick up your toys and move to another part of the playground.

Reserved gals need to widen their dating horizons, because this technique can work anywhere. Use your reserved personality to start rating everyone who passes by without saying a word. Then, like a homing pigeon, pick your target and move in for the "hover."

CEREBRAL

The cerebral personality is honestly the hardest type to meet men. If you are cerebral you can often give the appearance of having facts and figures in the front of your mind at all times: the expression on your face is not screaming, "Come meet me: I'm fun to be with." This makes it very hard for any man to make small talk with you, and even though small talk is not always fascinating, it is the first step toward developing a relationship.

Another strike against the cerebral woman is that most men operate in the primal state: they are hardwired to take on the alpha role in relationships. If you derail even the simplest conversation into a *National Geographic* documentary by showing off your stuff while he is talking, you will make him think that he is unimportant. It's not that I'm suggesting that you dull down your interests or analytical style, but you need to focus your facts on something relevant to the person standing in front of you.

My advice to Ms. Brainy is to get in touch with your emotional self when you are meeting new men. This is easier said than done for a girl who lives in her head, but I've found two great ways you can do this, and a third if you drink (though many brainy girls don't). The first way to get out of your head is to create physical stimulation. This will get someone's attention as well as allow you to explore other areas of yourself. When a man you are interested in approaches you, touch him ever so slightly while he is talking. You can shake his hand and hold it for a second longer than normal. You can graze his upper arm. You can poke him in the chest if he makes a joke. All of these techniques will lighten up the atmosphere as well as your facial expression and help you to connect with him in a way that says, "I want to be more than your mentor."

A second technique is to talk about your feelings instead of showing off what you know. You can use part of the basic feeling phrase, "I feel *blank*, when you say *blank*." Here's how it would look: "I felt good when you said you wanted to meet me." Saying how you feel will show off your softer side and for a smarty-pants like you, this is a good thing.

The third technique is to have a cocktail at home before you go out at night (note to self: designate someone else to be the driver or take public transportation when using this strategy). Sometimes all it takes is one glass of wine to loosen up a bit so that you don't seem uptight.

WHERE THE BOYS ARE

After you have practiced rating yourself and some unsuspecting guys near you, take your new system into the world but consider what you're looking for. Allow your number to steer you in the right direction.

First start with where you normally hang out. Are there any guys in your range in the places you frequent? If you don't get out much, and your only face time is at the grocery store or Blockbuster, then you better make it good. Start by shopping at stores that have the highest concentration of men in your range. Maybe it's the supermarket next to the big tech company, sports facility, gym, or office park. Spend the extra gas money and bring your coupons over there, instead of to the one you like that's near your house that has the great selection of yogurt. There are also certain times of the day when single guys are more prone to shop. Guys don't plan anything: they simply go to the grocery store at dinnertime to get something to eat for dinner. This is when you should be shopping, too. Save your dash for stocking up on Lean Cuisines and trash magazines for later in the night.

Movie stores are another great place for any type of woman to meet guys. But don't be hanging out in the drama section where the chick flicks are. Make yourself available first. Peruse the perimeters of the store where the "current releases" are stocked, or hang out in the action/adventure section. You can pick up your Emma Thompson film on the way out, after you've exchanged phone numbers.

No matter where you are going to shop for guys, keep your state of mind in check. Attracting men takes a little bit of work, as well as a game plan. You are leaving your home or office with a purpose, so get ready for it. Make sure you radiate your intention, which is to show the world that you are a great single woman. Your outfit should express this sentiment, as well as the expression on your face. If you look bothered, annoyed, or uptight, you are not going to attract anything besides pity.

It's not so much about where you go to meet men, as much as it is about being smart about the locale. Think about your normal routine. Where do you go? Where do you shop? Where do you eat? Are you hitting the cafeteria with the seniors at 5:00 P.M. because you can get a plate to take home? Why not hit the "heat and eat" aisle at your local supermarket at 7:00 P.M. and bump into testosterone-filled locals that were born in your century? Are you shopping for clothes at discount stores or hitting the women-only gym? Change it up a bit and open yourself up to meeting some new people. If you are going to mixers and cocktail parties just make sure that you are not in over your head or surrounded by men that don't rate the same as you. Positioning yourself in locations that reflect your rating is an important key to finding someone who you will match.

Work is a tricky place to date. The rule of thumb is that you don't date people you work with, and you especially stay clear of dating people you work for. However, you can date the friends of coworkers. If you rate your coworkers and find yourself compatible with some, ask them if they can fix you up with their friends. It's a long shot, but it may be worth the effort. One after-office happy hour never killed a person, especially when you are all allowed to bring your friends as well.

DON'T KEEP BAD COMPANY

I know you love your girls, but do you have to have them around all the time? Are they helping you find your perfect match? You don't have to drop them altogether but you should branch out. Your girls could be working against you, especially if they rate below you.

If your girlfriends rate below you then just by osmosis you could be attracting lower-scoring guys, thus thwarting your best efforts to meet someone who is compatible with you. It may feel great to be the good-looking friend in the group, but it could be hurting your chances of meeting your number. And don't think that hanging out with higher-number gal pals is the way to go, either. If you are out with a better-looking friend chances are she will be talking to guys that are way over your range, and you'll be playing wingman with a guy who has no interest in you.

My advice is when you are going out to meet guys, pick just one fem buddy who rates the same as you do to sweeten the pot. You don't have to ignore your other friends, but choose the time you spend with them wisely. Not every Friday night has to be "meet men night." But when you do go out with that goal in mind, spend time with your same-range friend so that you can share men in your range. It may seem like the competition would hurt your chances but this doesn't turn out to be the case. Most guys go out in pairs and sometimes in packs. Even if you are just going to the farmers' market bring a gal pal and increase your chances of getting Mr. Right Range to come chat.

LEAVING THE SCENE OF A CRIME

If you are seriously trying to find Mr. Right Range then don't waste time. If you've been invited to a friend's birthday, and you show up only to find three couples, two stragglers, and Rico Suave hitting on the hot waitress, lower your expectations of meeting someone, and try to have a great time anyway. But if you are at a party, club, or event and you've rated every single guy in the room and none match your score, then leave. The night is young: go and find somewhere else with fresh guys to rate. Make sure that you have enough cash on you so that you can throw down a $20 and make a quick getaway.

There is always somewhere else to go and more people to meet. I keep spare shoes in my car for just this reason. I put on my flats and go to a bookstore or coffee shop, or I change into my heels and go to a local pub or nightspot. If you can't think of anywhere to go, then go home and hit a park or gym the next morning. You are sure to see some guys there and you will be looking extra rested, too.

Michelle

Michelle is a divorced workaholic with a young son. Her project planning job keeps her tied to her phone, in late-night meetings, and out of the dating scene. When Michelle was finally ready to date she felt that she needed major help from her friends. She pried herself away from her responsibilities one night and went out to dinner with her best friend, Caitlin. Caitlin is married to a very busy doctor but loves to go out and matchmake.

As far as Michelle is concerned, Caitlin is the cutest, funniest person ever. Caitlin has been blessed with amazing looks, a great bod, and a personality that only sees the very best in people. During dinner Caitlin says that her hubby's best friend would be perfect for Michelle. Caitlin fished out a picture of a tall, dark, and handsome Duke University graduate named David. After some coaxing, Michelle agreed to meet him. With her busy schedule she had no idea when it would be possible.

A few days later Michelle got a call when she was headed home from a late meeting. It was Caitlin; she and David were going to a lounge to see David's brother perform. The lounge was on Michelle's way home, so she arranged for a baby-sitter and met them straight from the office. There he was in all his glory, better looking than the picture, laid-back, and really nice. Michelle rated him and the numbers didn't look good. The tall, athletic, single mom rated herself a grateful 8 but David rated a deserving 9. She knew immediately that this setup was not going to work, but instead of exiting stage right, Michelle lingered. Caitlin, who is always so positive, assured her she did a great job impressing David, but Michelle wasn't really surprised when he never called.

INTERNET DATING

The Rating Game is a must for Internet dating. Don't leave your relationships to be determined by computer programs. Whether you are using a matching site or just an introducing site you need to rely on the Rating Game and your Personal Filter to weed out all the Internet hits that you get or want to get.

The Internet has changed the scope of meeting people forever, and it has its good aspects, as well as some seriously scary flaws. While it is great to have the opportunity to chat with anyone anywhere in the world, some people use its anonymity to create new personas, or worse, stalk their victims. You have to be so careful when you are looking at the various dating sites, and take the high road whenever you can: go online and tell the truth about yourself. While people have been lying to each other since the beginning of time, the Internet has created a wild-and-out atmosphere. Worse, computer glitches, hiccups, and misinformation have been a continual source of contention. The computer programs create matches based on the input they are given. This is why it is so important to have checks and balances even within matchmaking sites and Internet dating sites. Rating your prospects is the final check in your system to finding a great relationship.

The first person you should know about when you begin Internet dating is yourself. Once you rate yourself, focus on responding to hits or contacting others that seem to be in your range. Instead of looking for one attribute or another, let an overall rating lead you to the person that will truly suit you.

The Rating Game is compatible with most Internet dating sites. You can rely on the dating site to introduce you to men, and then let the Rating Game help you sort them and figure out who is going to be worth your time. All Internet dating sites have their own personality but they operate on the same basic principles. They build up lists of registered members and then give them access to one another. The sites allow you to post certain information that either you choose or they extract through profile tests. The dating site not only has your interests in mind but also the interests of the men they are introducing you to.

The mission of the Internet dating site is to give all their clients enough prospects so that they will feel satisfied with the service, and recommend it to their friends. The site will be throwing men at you and trying to convince you to pursue them. Your job is to find the ones that will be right for you.

RATE YOURSELF ONLINE

The first step to integrating the Rating Game with an Internet site is to rate yourself according to my method. Then find a picture of yourself that you like for posting. You need a picture that looks like you on a good day: not your best, highest-rated day. We want to minimize the lying, but maximize your best aspects for the greatest impact.

Next, write a profile that expresses your rating. Go back to chapter 2 and look over your high, low, and average adjectives, and use them where appropriate in your description. The key is not to reveal too much in your profile. Share what you would normally say to someone in the first five minutes of meeting them. A polite social interaction would include what you do for a living, what part of town you live in, and what you like to do for fun. If you are filling out an in-depth profile test don't feel pressured into exposing the most intimate details of your life or your feelings. It may feel good to reveal yourself, but save it for the psychotherapy. Keep your answers brief and to the topmost layers of your personality and life situation. This will ensure that you don't overexpose yourself in the profile and that you will not feel a false sense of intimacy with anyone you are just meeting.

RATING INTERNET DATES

Now that your online persona echoes your real persona it is time to start rating potential matches. Most dating sites will have you log in to see a plethora of available men. Don't be surprised if you experience a sense of joy and stress at the same time: all of a sudden, there are tons of men to meet, but you don't know how you will sort them out.

That's where the Rating Game comes into play. You will break down these profiles into the same four categories. Grab a pencil and paper and create the Rating Game grid. Then, rate each of your potential matches based on the pictures they sent and their short blurb.

Even a short description is telling: "Professional M 32, seeks S, professional F on Westside." I would interpret this to say that this man's personality is straight/lackluster; he is proud of his home base. Couple that information with the scores you see from the picture, and you have got yourself a Rating Game score. Then decide which Internet matches are in the same range as you. The problem most people have dating online is similar to how they dated when we all were meeting face-to-face. They look at one attribute or another and don't see people as a whole. Or they try and find the guy with the most toys or who looks the best, and then are surprised when they are in over their head and completely out of their range.

WEBLATIONSHIPS

There are a couple of steps in between the initial profile view and meeting your match. Most of the time, initial contact is going to be made via e-mail. This is a time to let your true personality shine. You can make it clear that you are outgoing, flirty, reserved, or cerebral. Take your best shot at clever conversation. However, learning how to control your online intimacy will help you meet your match sooner.

When you think of the word "intimacy" you may be thinking about sex, but sex is just one aspect of this term. Think "into me see." Intimacy is a way of revealing yourself to another person and should be done in stages, and only when it is reciprocated. You don't want to reveal yourself at a pace online that you would feel comfortable doing in a relationship in the real world. Even in the "real world" many women reveal themselves, emotionally and physically, way too fast and at a pace that is unmatched by the men they date. They reveal more of themselves than the person they are with is ready to know about, which puts these women in a vulnerable position of giving without receiving. And because there are many ways to read into an e-mail, you don't want to give too much before you have an opportunity to get some information back.

Rate your match after your first e-mail. If he comes on too strong for you, take that into your rating score. If your ratings continue to match, then setting up a date is the next step. Meet your match somewhere public, do not invite him to your home. Remember, even if you have great e-mails back and forth, this man is a stranger to you until you meet him face-to-face. Choose somewhere you will be comfortable so that you will be at your best.

If all goes well, you're on your way to a full-fledged Weblationship. Rate yourself and your date at each milestone. For Internet dating, the milestones are profile, first e-mail, first phone call, first meeting, first date, three months, and six months.

INTERNET DATING SITES

Notice how these popular Internet dating sites have both pros and cons. Many people find these sites are very useful for meeting people. The Rating Game is completely compatible with any of these sites.

EHARMONY

eHarmony was one of the first online dating services that utilizes more than a picture and personality profile.

Pros

Matches you based on aspects of your personality. Has a high rate of people getting married from introductions on their site.

Cons

Matches are based on similar attributes and based on the founder's moral code. If you have the same ideals as Neil Clark Warren you have a very high chance of getting hitched. However, if you differ you might feel like you are getting the e-scraps instead of eHarmony.

MATCH

With more than twenty million members Match.com is the largest online dating site, giving it the ability to introduce you to more people in your area.

Pros

Match.com lets you post up to twenty-five pictures.

Cons

The extensive list of members and match availability can be overwhelming. This site will give you the ability to meet many people but be careful, because more pictures can sometimes mean that people are focused just on your looks.

CHEMISTRY

This site matches people based on a personality profile. This is the only site that claims to match you based on chemistry.

Pros

Predicts future matches based on the choices you made in your previous matches.

Cons

People you date can post feedback on you online for future daters to read. This TiVolike program can grow with your choices but doesn't leave room for an eclectic blend of styles.

PERFECTMATCH

This site employs the patented Duet test to send you matches that match your profile and your own criteria.

Pros

The lengthy profile system tends to weed out those not wanting a serious relationship.

Cons

Initial profile takes a long time to fill out. This lengthy survey takes out some of the mystique involved with getting to know a person.

LAVALIFE

Lavalife is a phone, e-mail, and text-based personal ad. You can post voice mail, send e-mails, or text local singles.

Pros

Works well for people who prefer voice communication.

Cons

Easier access to other applicants raises the risk factor.

E-TRAMPS

You don't leave your heart or emotions behind when you go on-line, so protect yourself the same way you would in real life. If you think it would be a bad idea to start intimate relationships with a dozen guys at the same time in real life, then it is a bad idea to do it online. If you would casually meet and greet half a dozen men in a week in real life, then treat your online matches the same. You don't want to become an e-tramp, stringing along dozens of men at the same time. On the flip side, you don't want to be pouring your heart out to every guy with a profile, either.

E-tramps put too much out there, too soon, and to too many people. Communication should be reciprocal, which means that you should give a little and receive a little over time. If you are giving a lot to numerous people at the same time you are devaluing what you have to offer and will in turn feel that down the line.

RATING GAME MILESTONES

There are several crossroads in a relationship where you should stop and reassess: use the Rating Game to see how things are going and if you are still the strong match you were when the relationship began.

THE FIRST FIVE MINUTES

You will be able to get a rating from a guy after chatting for five minutes. Read into the conversation and don't be afraid to ask questions. The face and body area will come instantly. Personality will also show itself pretty quickly. The one that might take a little more decoding is life situation. You may have to use clues from what he says to figure out what his life situation is like. What he does for a living will tell you a lot. If he's a teacher he probably stays at home at night grading papers. If he's a cop he probably spends lots of time at the gym and working odd hours. Recreation and hobbies can also say a lot: if he likes one-on-one sports he probably likes to spend time alone.

FIRST DATE

Rerate after your first date. You will know more about him after you see how he picks you up or meets your friends. Is he late, does he flake, or does he try to reschedule? You'll also learn a lot more about his personality and life situation. Consider where he lives, who he lives with, if he has pets, where he works, if he travels, and where he likes to hang out.

The best part about the Rating Game on a first date is that you are considering how all of his attributes work together. He is not just a funny guy, good-looking, hot body, or cool car, he is a combination of all of his attributes and this is when you can really find out if you match. Remember if you think he is better than you, then move on. You don't want to be with someone who thinks they can do better, or vice versa. You don't want to be with a fixer-upper, either. Remember, you cannot magically turn him into the person you need him to be. If the numbers don't add up the way you intended, make it a quick date and move on.

THREE MONTHS

You are about to cross the point of no return. After three months, it is unlikely that you will be able to get out of this relationship without getting hurt or hurting him. If you are passing the three-month mark it means that you are officially dating: this is definitely more than just a fling. It's time to rerate and make sure that you are dating someone that you are suited for.

SIX MONTHS

The six-month marker is when the heart is firmly attached or his habits get annoying. Unless the guy has a parole officer he didn't tell you about or suddenly tells you that he wants you to move to a polygamist camp, chances are that you have already seen the writing on the walls. If you sense that this guy is not for you but you've let yourself get attached anyway, rerate to confirm your suspicions. Let every fight, and every hurtful disappointment remind you that your numbers don't match and get out before you end up getting more involved.

The happy side of rerating is that you very well may find that none of these problems occurred, and that the system worked! You found someone that is perfect for you, even after you've learned where he keeps his dirty socks. Congratulate yourself for choosing well and sticking with it. This one might be a keeper.

Sonia

The sweltering heat and humidity had finally run their course, and Sonia found herself enjoying the sunset backstage at a concert in Lake Texoma. The young emcee had twisted her hair up and her white sundress blew in the sudden cool air. It was almost time for the last band when she spotted a handsome roadie. Mark was touring with one of the bands. He had found several reasons to talk to Sonia before she realized she was the object of his eye. She noticed for the rest of the night that his glances began and ended with her.

Sonia spent time with the band after the show and Mark hung out with her crew in the following days. She enjoyed getting to know Mark but assumed it would quickly end when they left the lake: Sonia lived in the northern part of the state while Mark was a local. Though it was long distance the two spoke every day. Sonia rated the two and even though they got their points in very different ways they both rated in the same range.

	Sonia	Mark
Face	8	7
Body	7	8
Personality	8	8
Life situation	6	8
OVERALL=	7.25	7.75

Mark joked nonstop but was very serious about his feelings for Sonia. He had some time off and wanted to see her again. His first visit was slightly delayed but their connection when he arrived was instant. The two had so much fun that she was willing to overlook his delay and a third-wheel friend that traveled with him.

Sonia was so excited about seeing him again that for his next visit she rearranged her schedule. Then the day before his visit he told her he wouldn't be able to make it. She was disappointed but understood that sometimes things happen. Then he told her he was going to Houston with a friend for a football game and she was upset.

The final blow was when she went to visit him. He started the weekend off by arriving late at the airport because he was having dinner with a friend. He immediately ushered her into a group of all his friends and they spent almost no time alone together to reconnect. He worked for most of the following day and picked her up late again. The whole weekend was a bust.

When she got home Sonia rerated Mark and found that their numbers had changed. His personality had some serious flaws and his life situation was mostly fluff. Upon a closer look she realized that even though he seemed totally into her, he wasn't reliable. She also saw how his job controlled his life. She still liked him but with his unreliability, the numbers just didn't add up for them anymore.

	Sonia	Mark
Face	8	7
Body	7	8
Personality	8	4
Life situation	6	4
OVERALL=	7.25	5.75

DON'T RATE YOUR MATE

The Rating Game is for dating relationships, not committed relationships. Stop rating once you hear the word "commitment." This can come any time, but usually I've found that it follows shortly after the six-month marker. And once you have reached this stage, it's time to shelf the Rating Game. If you have made a commitment to a relationship then you need to honor that commitment by trying to make it work, regardless of your ratings. It no longer matters what you rate: it's much more important to make sure that you are both happy and thriving as partners, and looking forward to the future without apprehension.

There are two different types of commitments. The most basic commitment is to not see other people. If you have committed to not see other people then that means not rating other prospects. If you truly want to know what else is out there then you should redefine your current relationship first. Dating works on the honor system, and you'll feel better about yourself if you keep your head in the game one guy at a time. If you are thinking about rating other people, then chances are that you've outgrown the relationship you are currently in.

A step up from exclusive is a relationship that is committed to the long term. This is the modern-day "promise ring." Being committed to someone means that you are devoted to working through problems. Every relationship will have difficult times but being in a long-term relationship means that you are ready and willing to work through them.

You know that you're in a committed relationship when:

• You are exclusively dating each other

• You are in his speed dial or top five

• You have developed pet names for each other and you can't remember why

• You know all the names of his family members, going back to second cousins

• Jewelry has been exchanged

• His mother/sister calls you when they are looking for him

8.

Reba's Eleventh Commandment
Thou Shalt Not Rub It in Their Faces

THE RATING GAME is like having the secret superhero power of dating discernment: it protects you from getting involved in doomed relationships. You will never feel rejected when you find out that someone's number is higher than yours, because you can choose not to start something in the first place. You don't have to give every guy with "potential" a chance date just in case he could be "the one"—the numbers will work that out for you. *But with great power comes great responsibility, so you need to use the Rating Game wisely and responsibly.*

There are going to be times when you are tempted to share your ratings with your family, friends, or even the men you rate. I suggest you resist this temptation. While it is fun to rate your date, you should keep this pleasure all to yourself. There is absolutely nothing wrong with a little personal pleasure. Pull out your cell phone calculator and click away, but don't share your results. The purpose of the Rating Game is to decide if you should pursue someone that you are attracted to. It is not supposed to provide ammunition to make anyone feel superior, and consequently make others feel bad about themselves. That's why my Eleventh Commandment is, "Thou shalt not rub it in their faces."

The Rating Game is a great tool that can keep people from getting hurt; it shouldn't be used as a vehicle to hurt others. The truth is painful, especially when it's boiled down to a single number. It's also very misleading to share your composite score with another person without being able to fully express exactly how you came to that number. For example, I once told a friend his score, and it was devastating. You can't imagine the look of hurt in his eyes when I told him he was almost a 7, when by his calculations, he was a serious contender for an 8. The difference in the outcome was directly related to my Personal Filter: what was "good" for me was considered "great" by him. I started to dig myself out of this hole by telling him, in detail, where the differences in our scores came from, but no car ride home could possibly be long enough to explain why I rated him as I did. Not to mention the fact that it was totally awkward to talk about his body and face. In the end, there was no saving the situation, and I know that it permanently affected our friendship. Imagine what this information could do to a dating relationship?

There is a temptation to tell someone when they score high, but you can hurt them with a high number just like you can with a low number. You can lull a man into a false sense of security if he doesn't feel comfortable with himself. Worse, the next person that comes along could rate him completely differently. In your mind he is a 9, but to another person he is a 7, or even a 4 to himself.

The bottom line is that the score you give someone else should not matter to anyone but yourself. Instead, it's the number they rate themselves that they need to justify or live with. If he's happy being a 4, more power to him. If he's not happy with a 4, chances are he might just change his rating with a little homework. Then, the cute 4 you were keeping in your hip pocket just may transform into someone that is way out of your league.

While it can be fun to "kiss and tell" with your girlfriends, sharing the way you rate a date won't make much sense to them, either. Your rating scale is based on so many personal factors that it becomes relatively meaningless to anyone else. And, you may not want to share your sordid past with anyone else, even your best friends. And if you share your ratings with your friends, don't be surprised if they don't agree: you may give his thin physique a 6 and she may give it an 8. Your girlfriends may rate you a 9 when you only rate yourself a 7. At the end of the day the only opinion that is important is your own.

ENDING A RELATIONSHIP WITH CLASS

If you see that a relationship is heading south, and the Rating Game confirms your suspicions, use your secret power to end the romance as quickly as possible. With the power of the Rating Game, you'll have the conviction to cut him loose. I like to do it the *Seinfeld* way, "One motion, right off."

Ending a relationship early is key to the Rating Game. When there is less emotional attachment, it's easier to do the dumping. Use the Rating Game to end any bad relationship, at any stage. If your prospect is not in the same range as you, then don't pursue him, no matter how easy it looks. If you've gone out on a few dates and know the numbers don't match up, all you are doing by sticking it out is creating another bad relationship. They say you need twenty-one days to make a habit or break a habit. Are you talking to Mr. Wrong on the phone every night or getting used to the sound of your phone alerting you to a text message during the day? You could be building a habit that's going to leave you unable to sleep without a call from him, or your thumbs twitching to text. The easiest way to break a habit is to never make it.

Just because you are the one doing the dumping doesn't mean that it's easy to leave a relationship. You can start to feel like a monster for breaking so many hearts. My advice is the sooner you end a relationship that you know is not going to make you happy the less people will get hurt. As you rate and date you will feel more confident that the numbers really do dictate how a relationship will end up, and then you will be able to end it before anyone gets too involved. Besides, sometimes guys expect to strike out, and are really surprised when they don't.

Breaking up can also make you lose hope that there is someone out there that can satisfy you. I know it's hard to face after a relationship fizzles, but the fact of the matter is that there are millions of men out there, and more than one of them is the right guy for you. If you refocus on your Personal Filter and figure out what you want in life right now, use the Rating Game as one of your many tools to get it. When you are happy with your numbers you'll know that you're ready to get back out there.

But because you can't throw their number in their face as a reason to get out, as in, "Sorry, but you're a 6 and I'm really looking for an 8," use one of the letdowns from this list. It's tempting to view men like a mango in the produce section, picking past the bruised fruit with not more than a glance. But don't. If relationships are about giving and growing then you need to recognize that all men have real feelings just like you. A little kindness goes a long way.

For best results, try to match each situation with the right category:

When Approached in a Public Space
- No, thank you
- I don't date people from _____ (work, the gym, and so on)
- The classic turn and walk away

After One Bad Date
- One date doesn't obligate me to answer the phone
- I've got a lot of other things going on right now
- I think of you more like a (sweet, annoying, or protective) brother

After Three Dates
- I'm still not over my ex
- The chemistry is just not there
- I thought things would be different with us

Passing After a Setup
- We seem to be at different places right now
- I don't think we have much in common
- I'm really busy at work this month

When He Can't Take the Hint
- I'm seeing someone
- No means no
- I'm calling security!

CONGRATULATIONS, GRADUATE!

If you're worried about how to turn men down, then you've come a long way, baby! I hope this method has helped you regain your confidence so that you can feel good about yourself and the men out there who are ready to date you. The lessons from the Rating Game can help you revamp your whole outlook on dating. You now know everything there is to learn about why people date to how they date. You have taken a holistic look at yourself and discovered exactly what it takes to be the best person you can be. If you've rated yourself successfully and started rating men, you're practically a pro. Within seconds you can tell if a relationship is going to be balanced or a flop. You are now ready for the Rating Game Dating Oath:

I pledge to rate the four areas of my life to achieve my overall rating and to do the same for the men I meet. I will not let myself fall for men who rate below me no matter how safe it feels. I will not allow myself to be tempted by men who rate above me no matter how flattering it may be. I promise to uphold the Eleventh Commandment by not revealing my rating or those that I rate. I commit to honor my future relationships by not rating my mate. I declare that I will use my Personal Filter and this rating system to make the choices that I know suit me best. I am determined to find a man in my range so that I can have a relationship that allows me the opportunity to give and to grow.

Saran

Before Saran learned how to play the Rating Game she was very confused about how she would make it in the dating world. She recognized that her greatest strength was her style and charm, but she also knew that her immigrant status kept her out of range for the guys she seemed attracted to. Saran had a unique international flair that always got her a foot in the door with successful businessmen, but once they learned that she worked at a local gas station to make money under the table, it was, as they say, "game over."

Saran came from a wealthy Mongolian family who sent her to the United States to attend college. However, during her junior year her mother passed away, and she had to go back to Mongolia for the funeral. She returned to the States too heartbroken to finish school. Unfortunately, her visa was directly related to school attendance. Without the desire to continue her education, Saran has been living in fear of extradition and scraping by with odd jobs.

I met Saran five years after her mother passed away; she was still trying to figure out where she fit into the bigger picture. I recognized that Saran could benefit from the Rating Game in many ways. Not only would it help her find the right guys to date, but it might give her the ability to take a hard look at her life and help get her back on track. After learning the rules of the Rating Game, and working out the numbers for herself, Saran realized that her life situation was pulling her overall score down. Saran gave herself a 7 for face, a 7 for body, an 8 for personality, but a 3 for life situation.

Saran and I worked out a plan to improve her life situation. We counted up all her existing credits and found that she was only one year away from achieving a bachelor's degree in marketing. I explained to Saran that even if she wasn't interested in working in the business world, a college degree was worth having, no matter what career she wanted to pursue. Saran told me that she really wanted to become a professional stylist. We agreed that the best way to meet her goals would be to enroll at a local beauty school while she was finishing up her college studies. Within six months she was putting on hair shows at the best salon in Seattle. She was able to use her marketing knowledge and charm to grow her business, and she even got the hair salon to sponsor her visa. When we reran her numbers, her life situation points increased to 6, increasing her overall score from a 6.25 to a solid 7.

About the same time, Saran connected with another stylist, José, in her shop. The two began dating. While she never expected to settle down with a stylist, she realized that she and José got along well. Saran rated José and found that they rated the same. She was ecstatic! Even though they came from different cultures and came to each other from very different paths they fit together beautifully.

In the beginning of their relationship Saran asked me what she should do if she met a more "successful" man, like the bankers she dreamed of dating. I reminded her of numbers, and the tons of bankers who had already dumped her, and how perfect José and she were together. It never took much to help her stay the course, and did it ever pay off.

Saran left Mongolia as a nineteen-year-old teenager with hopes of pleasing her parents. She returned to her county seven years later as a bride who had seen the world through the eyes of grief, guilt, hard work, and now love. José and Saran were married on that trip. As her father walked her down the aisle she knew that the road she had taken was not the one she had planned, but it ended up better than she could have ever imagined. She had made her family proud and found the love of her life, too!